AF379422

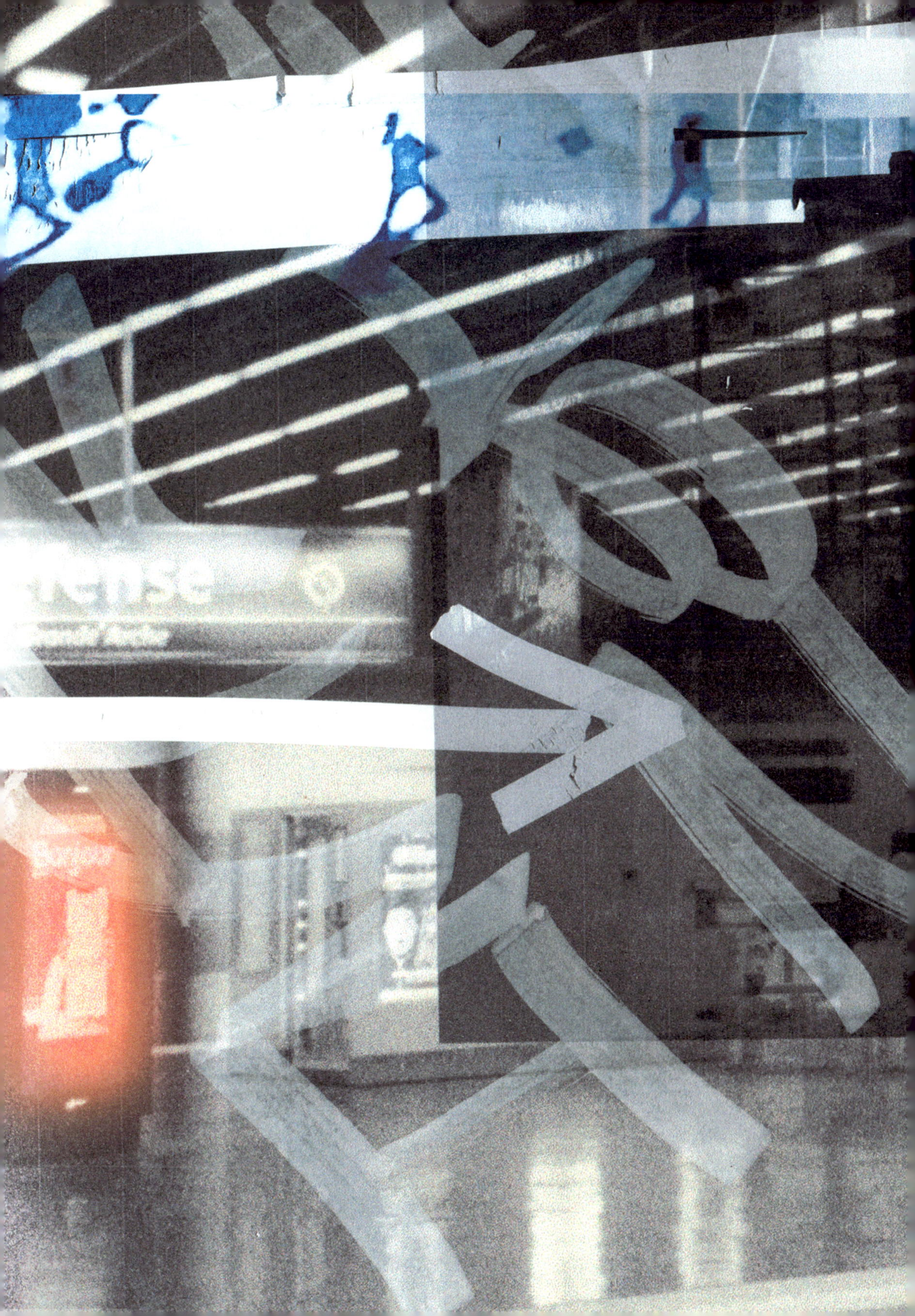

Contents

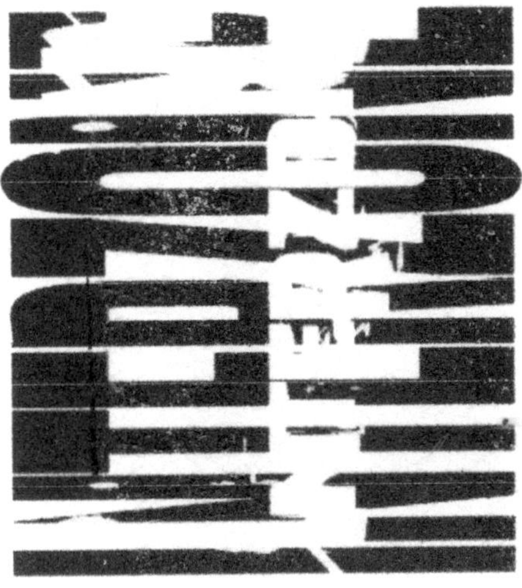

INTERZONE

interzone

A Topography of Power:
Valentin Noujaïm's *La Défense* Trilogy

Mohamed Almusibli

When I invited Valentin Noujaïm to realize his first institutional solo exhibition at Kunsthalle Basel, it was with the conviction that his work articulates something urgently needed in the present: a form of storytelling that does not merely seek visibility for the marginalized, but exposes the structures that obscure them. *La Défense*, Noujaïm's ambitious film trilogy, is such a work. Premiered in full for the first time as part of his exhibition *PANTHEON*, it is more than a cinematic cycle; it is a study in how spaces remember, forget, and suppress. Set against the architectural sprawl of Europe's largest business district, *La Défense* reclaims the symbolic and material terrain of the French Republic's most emblematic urban monument.

In naming the trilogy after this site, Noujaïm positions his project at the intersection of architecture, memory, and political refusal. The business district of La Défense, conceived in the 1960s as a beacon of progress and modernity, stands atop a literal and figurative burial ground: a former shantytown inhabited by Algerian workers whose histories are largely absent from France's official narrative. Across the three films, titled *Pacific Club* (2022), *To Exist Under Permanent Suspicion* (2024), and *Demons to Diamonds* (2025), Noujaïm constructs a cinematic counter-monument, one that honors not heroic myths, but lived precarity and survival.

Pacific Club, a film that reconstructs a nightclub once frequented by youth from the banlieues during the volatile 1980s, opens underground. Through the recollections of protagonist Azedine Benabdelmoumene, this vanished space is conjured not as nostalgia, but as testimony: a fragile sanctuary against the tide of institutional neglect. The film's quiet memories are set against the era's louder backdrop: the AIDS crisis, the heroin epidemic, the rise of the far right.[1] While the Pacific Club offered fleeting community, the French state unveiled the Grande Arche at La Défense, a towering, pristine monument to liberty and progress.[2] Noujaïm positions these gestures side by side: one intimate and imperiled,

1. See Didier Lestrade, *Act Up, une histoire* (Paris: Denoël, 2000) for a detailed account of the AIDS crisis in France and its intersections with immigrant communities and public discourse.

2. See Kristin Ross, *Fast Cars, Clean Bodies: Decolonization and the Reordering of French Culture* (Cambridge, MA: MIT Press, 1995).

the other monumental and abstract. The gap between them defines the trilogy's stakes.

To Exist Under Permanent Suspicion moves into a sterile corporate interior where surveillance supplants celebration. Claire, a young executive, is rendered legible through systems designed to dehumanize her. The glass offices she navigates are spaces of not only labor, but erasure. Her transformation from compliant employee to incendiary figure is portrayed not as pathology, but as a final act of presence. Within Noujaïm's frame, monstrosity becomes a form of resistance. The title underscores the ontological nature of the violence at play: To exist under such conditions is already to be marked, suspect, policed.[3]

The final film, *Demons to Diamonds*, finds the district speaking through silence. Echoes rise from underground as recurring suicides begin to haunt the narrative, not as anomalies but as indictments. The glass towers, emblems of success, fracture into scenes of isolation, their reflective surfaces now trapping rather than projecting. Each window contains a life sealed off from the others, an ecosystem of anxiety and paralysis. The promise of ascent is inverted. What once symbolized aspiration now stages a perpetual fall.

Noujaïm's formal vocabulary resists easy classification. Shot on 16mm film and enriched with CGI, archival textures, and layered sound design, the trilogy oscillates between memory and hallucination, history and dream. This hybridity is not a flourish; it is fundamental to his political aesthetic. These are stories that exist only in fragments, because fragmentation is the condition of their survival. The trilogy does not reconstruct a lost narrative; it attends to its remains.

The protagonists, like the figures evoked in journalist and literary critic Louisa Yousfi's notion of *héros du néant* (heroes of nothingness), are not restored to grandeur.[4] They endure at the margins of official history. In their refusal to disappear, they make visible the very mechanisms that would erase them. Noujaïm does not mythologize them. Instead, he traces their contours in flicker and shadow, insisting that their partial visibility is not a lack, but a critical stance.

3. Simone Browne, *Dark Matters: On the Surveillance of Blackness* (Durham, NC: Duke University Press, 2015).

4. Louisa Yousfi, *Rester barbare* (Paris: La Fabrique Éditions, 2021).

Taken together, the trilogy functions as a cinematic counter-monument. Whereas state monuments stabilize meaning and enshrine coherence, Noujaïm's films destabilize and complicate. They inhabit thresholds: between belonging and banishment, witness and absence, sound and silence. These are not merely thematic poles, but spatial and political coordinates. In Judith Butler's terms, they map a zone of "precarious life" where recognition must be fought for rather than granted.[5]

5. Judith Butler, *Precarious Life: The Powers of Mourning and Violence* (London: Verso, 2004).

That La Défense should be the site of this reckoning is no accident. It was built to embody postwar France's ideals of progress and integration, yet Noujaïm's trilogy reveals the cost of those ideals: displacement, invisibility, a carefully managed forgetting. By staging this cinematic intervention within that geography and by presenting it here, within Kunsthalle Basel's own architectural frame, we hope to draw attention to politics of space, image, and memory. Noujaïm's work challenges us to reimagine not only what stories we tell, but how and for whom they are told.

INTERZONE, the artist's book accompanying *PANTHEON*, assumes the guise of a fevered object: an uncanny dossier or speculative notebook imagined as authored by the mad architect of La Défense. Co-conceived by Valentin Noujaïm and designer Kim Coussée, its form mimics the fragmented, recursive logic of obsession. Film stills, annotated images, marginalia, and archival debris spiral into a structure that resists order, as if the book were unearthed from the rubble of a forgotten urban delirium. It is both document and hallucination, a narrative device where the topographies of memory, surveillance, and spectral presence begin to blur. A newly commissioned essay by writer Perwana Nazif threads through this apparatus like a fugue, drawing on philosophy, mysticism, and post-catastrophic thought to reflect on what is lost in the image, what resists inscription, and how Noujaïm's works inhabit the space between dream, death, and history's silences. Published in collaboration with Mousse Publishing, *INTERZONE* is not a supplement to the trilogy but a spectral extension of it, an object haunted by the same ghosts and complicit in the same refusal to forget.

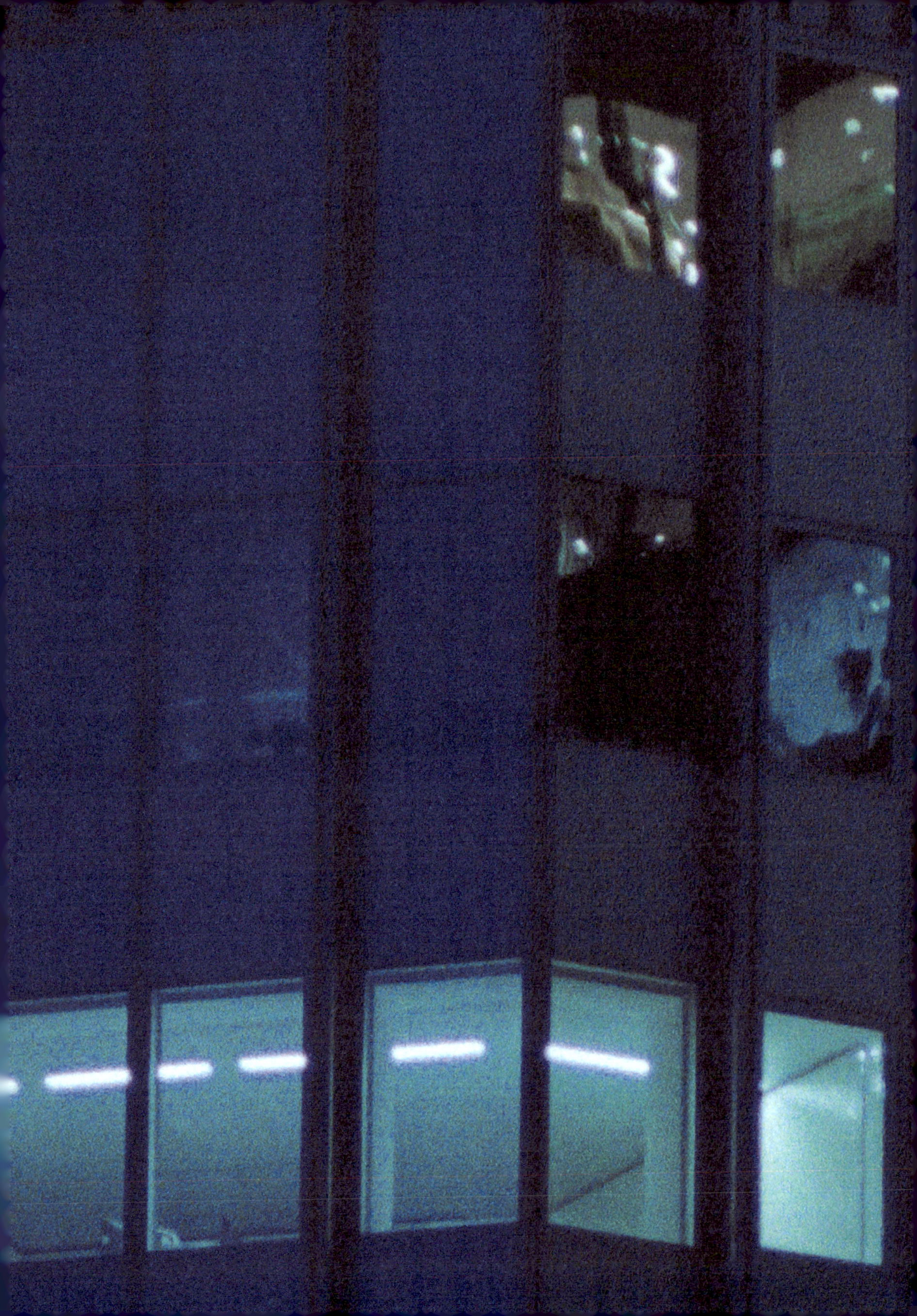

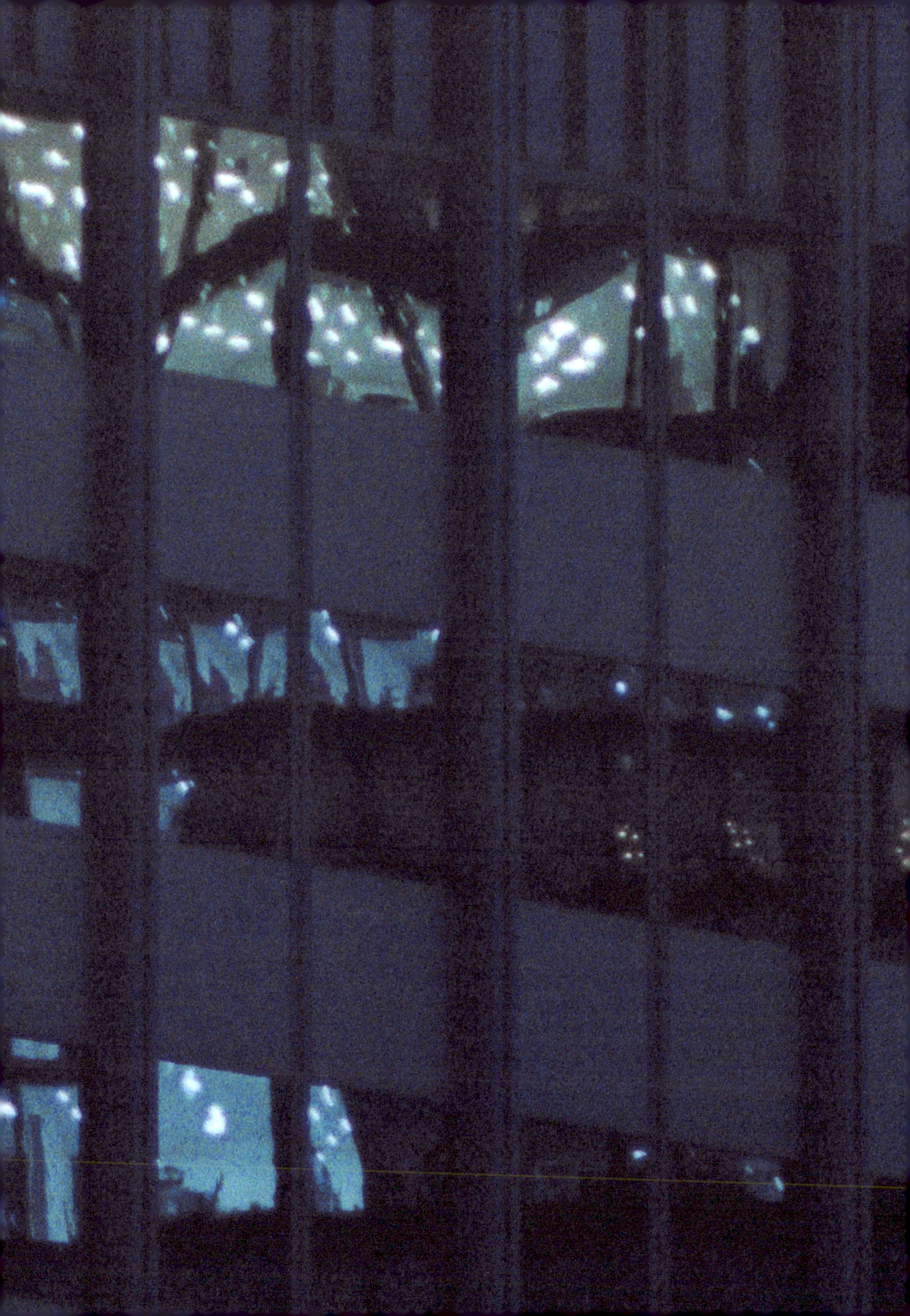

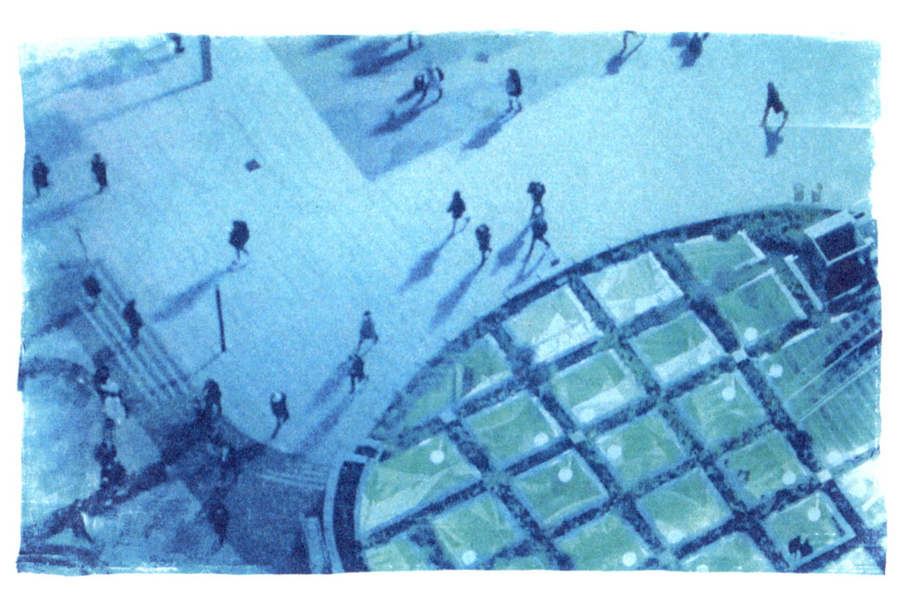

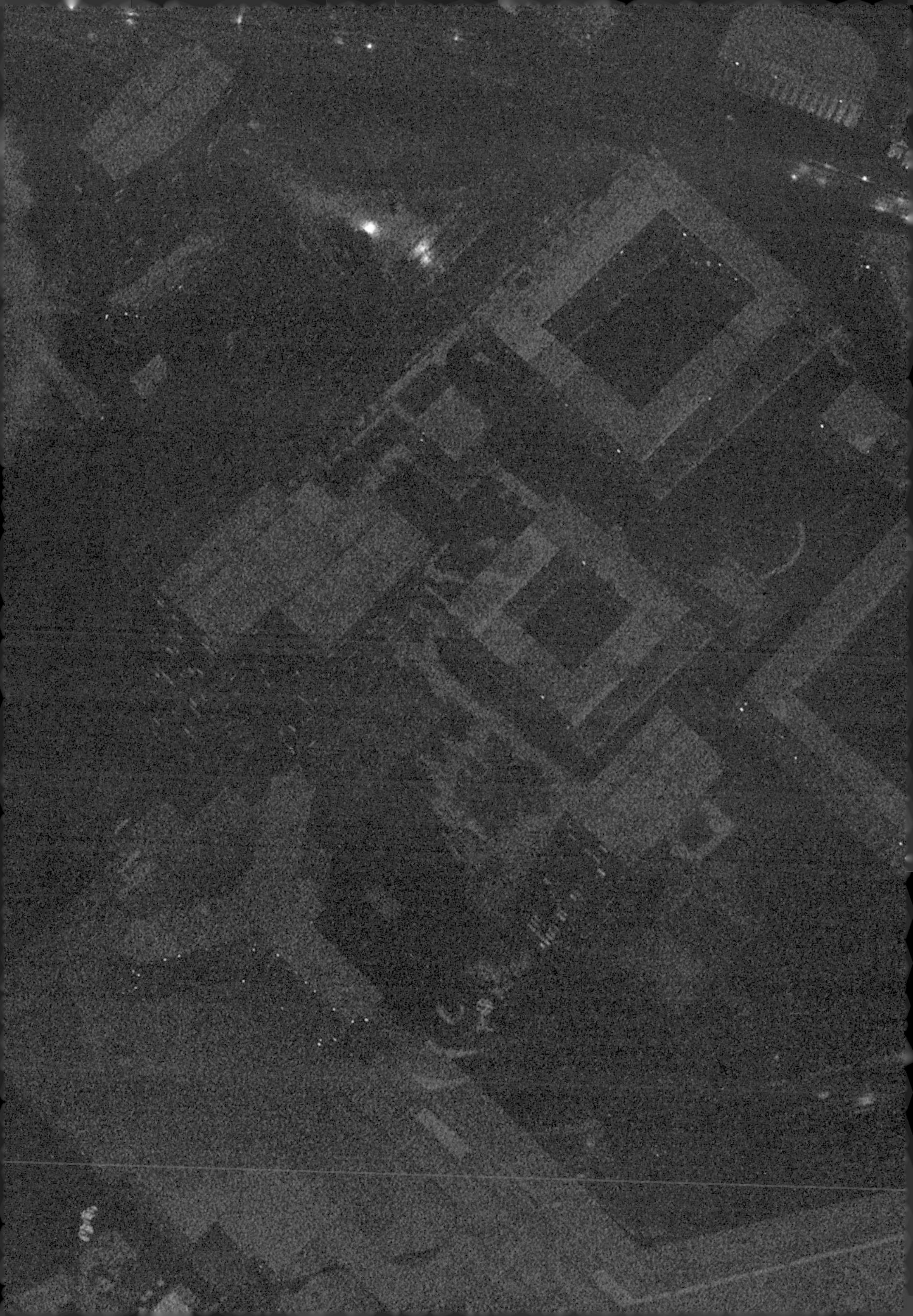

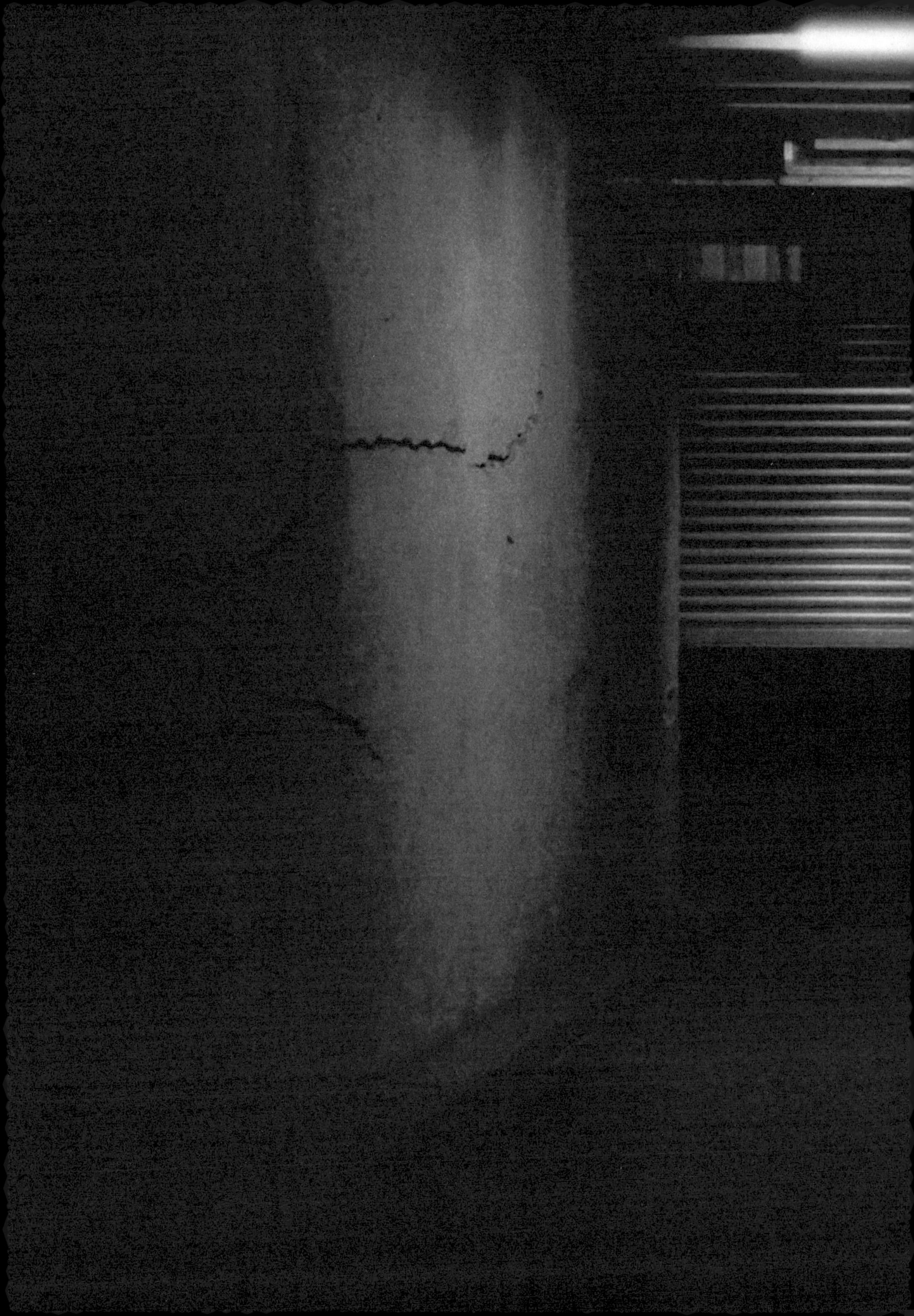

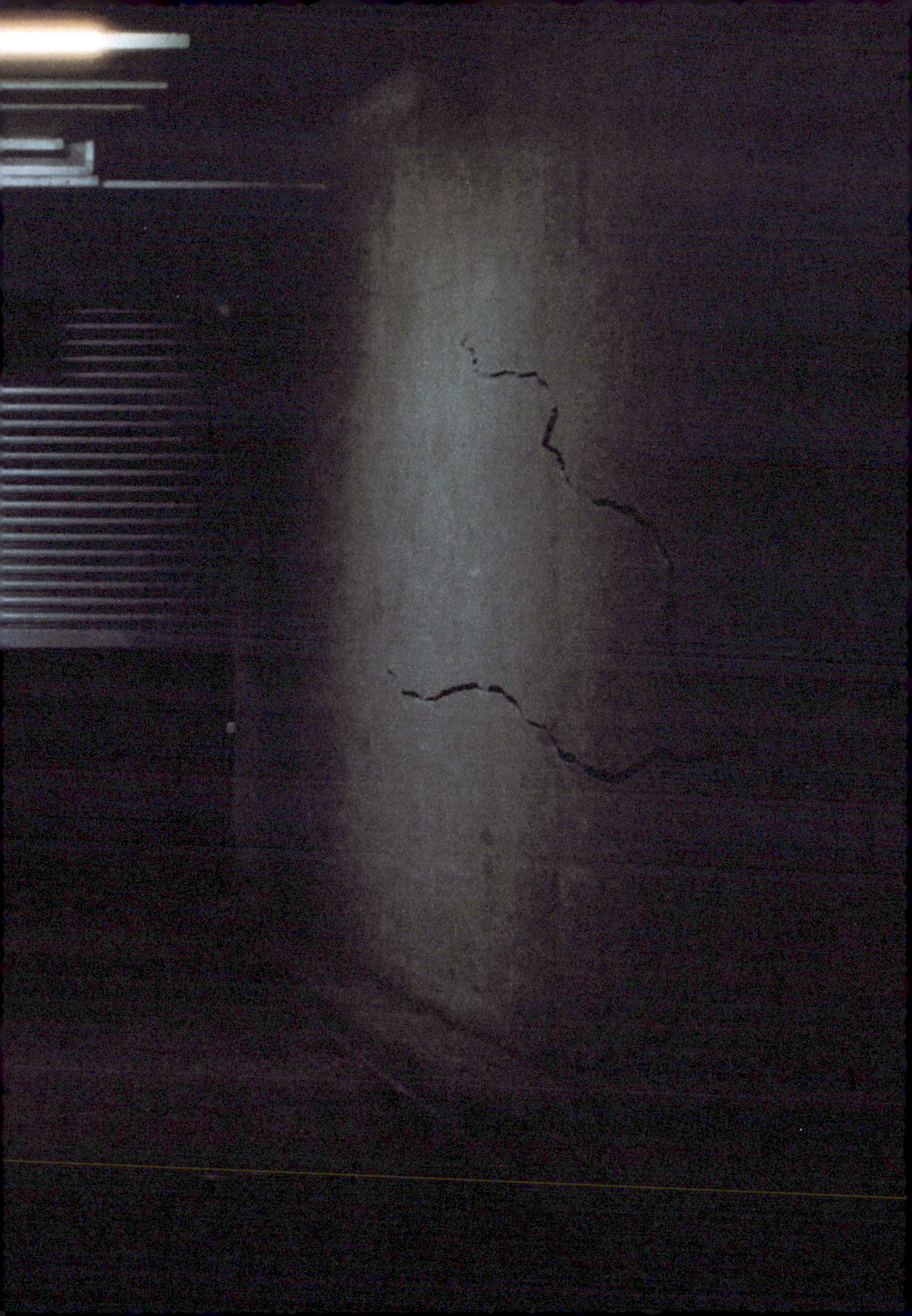

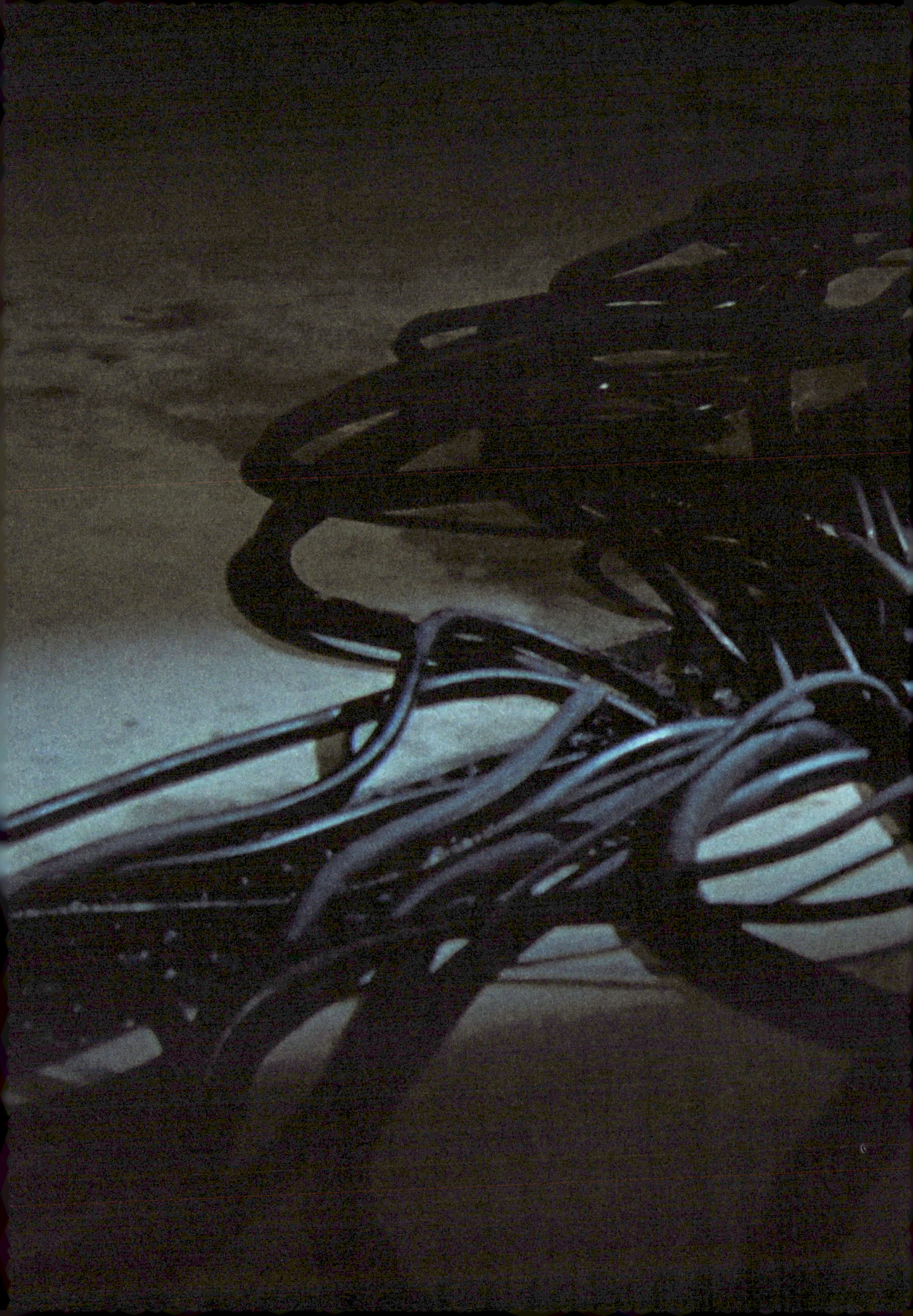

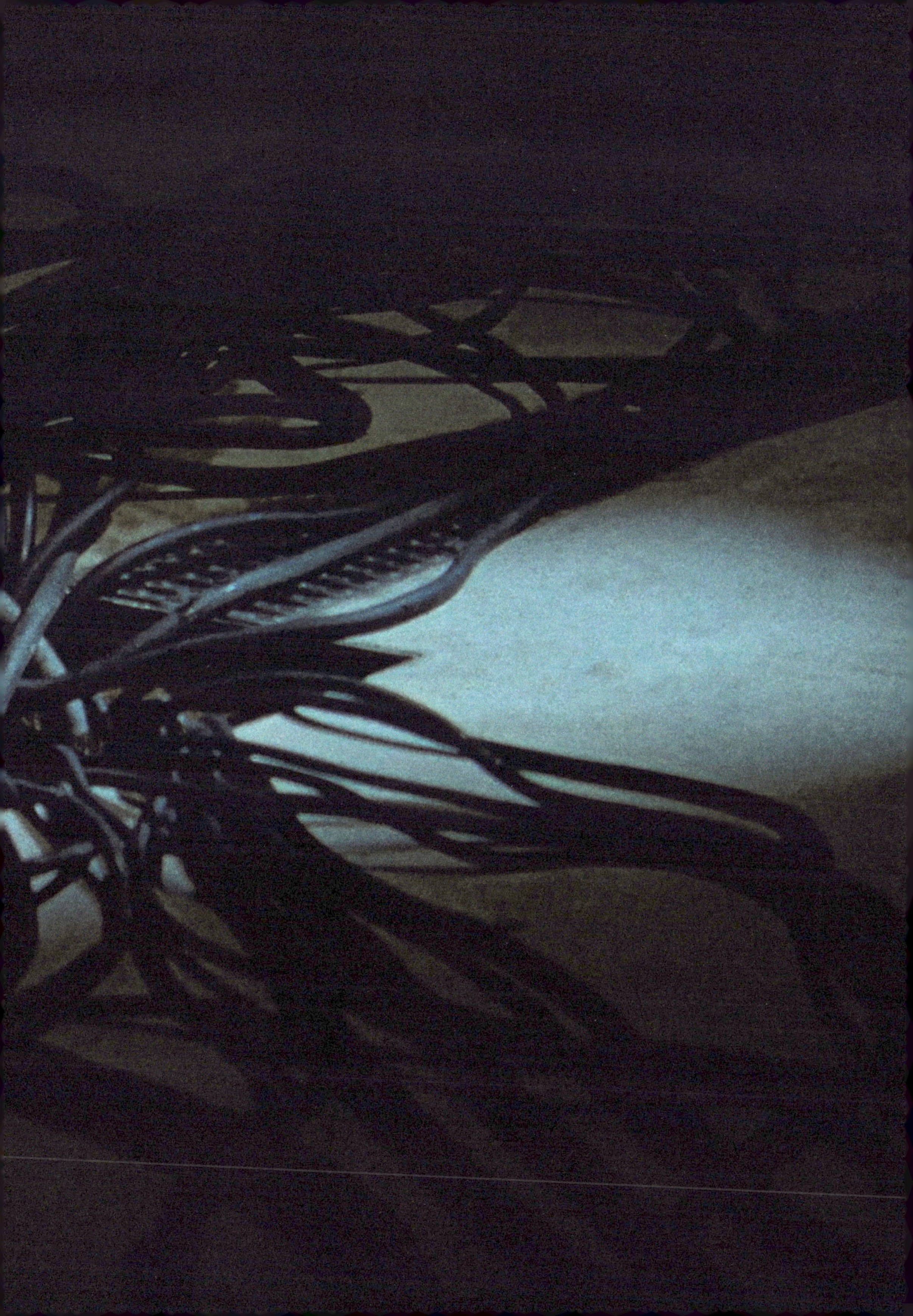

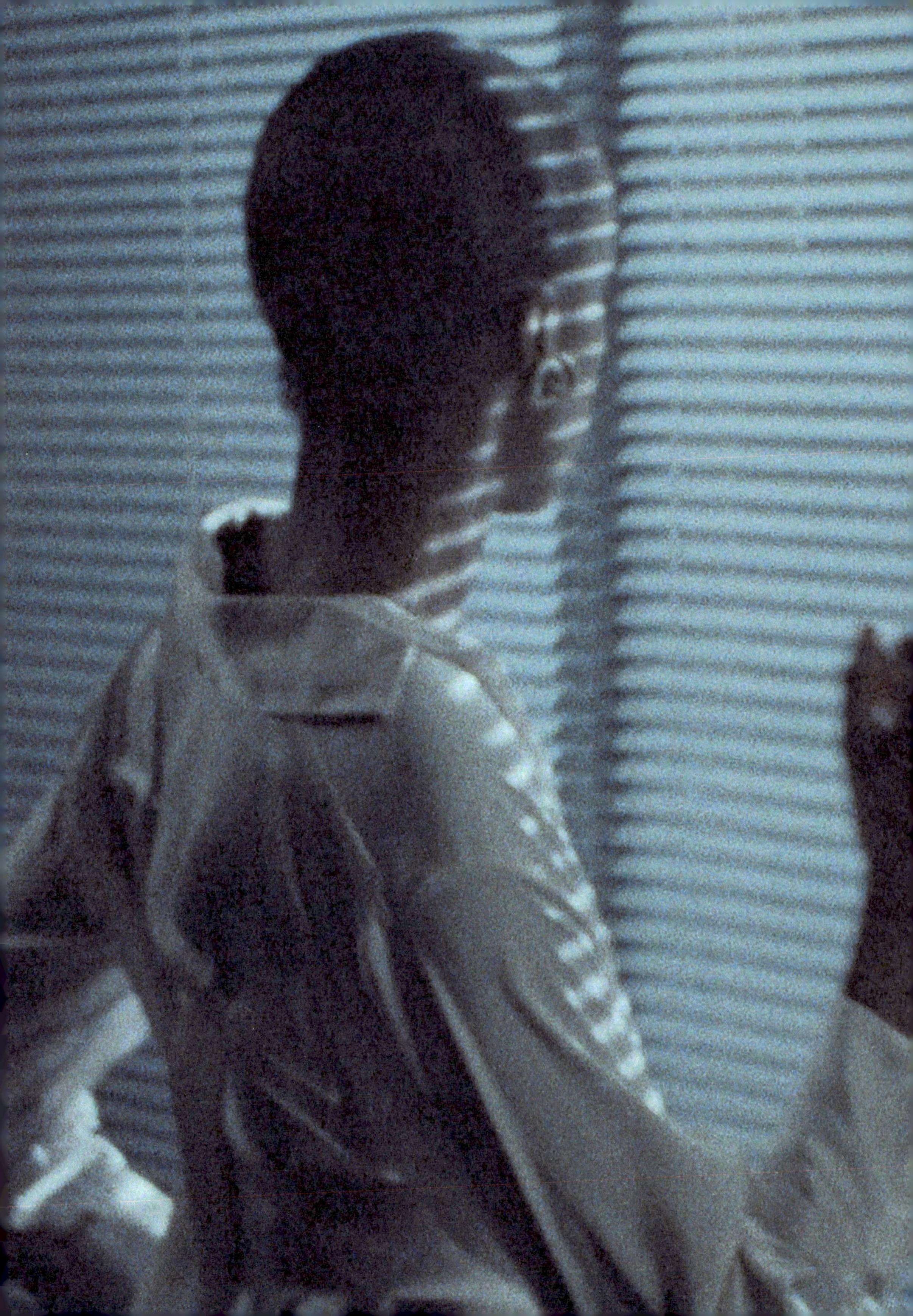

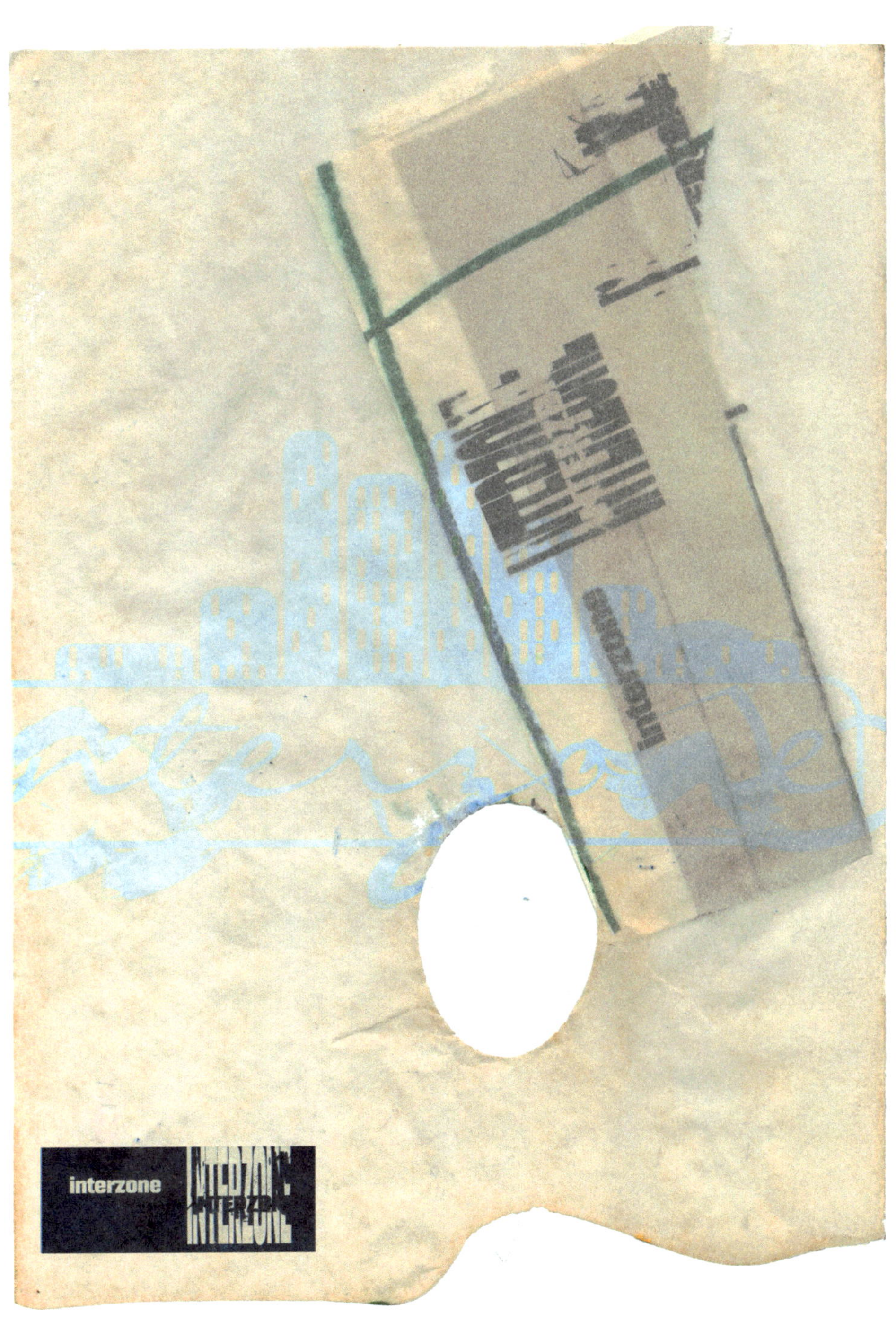

interzone
INTERZONE
INTERZONE

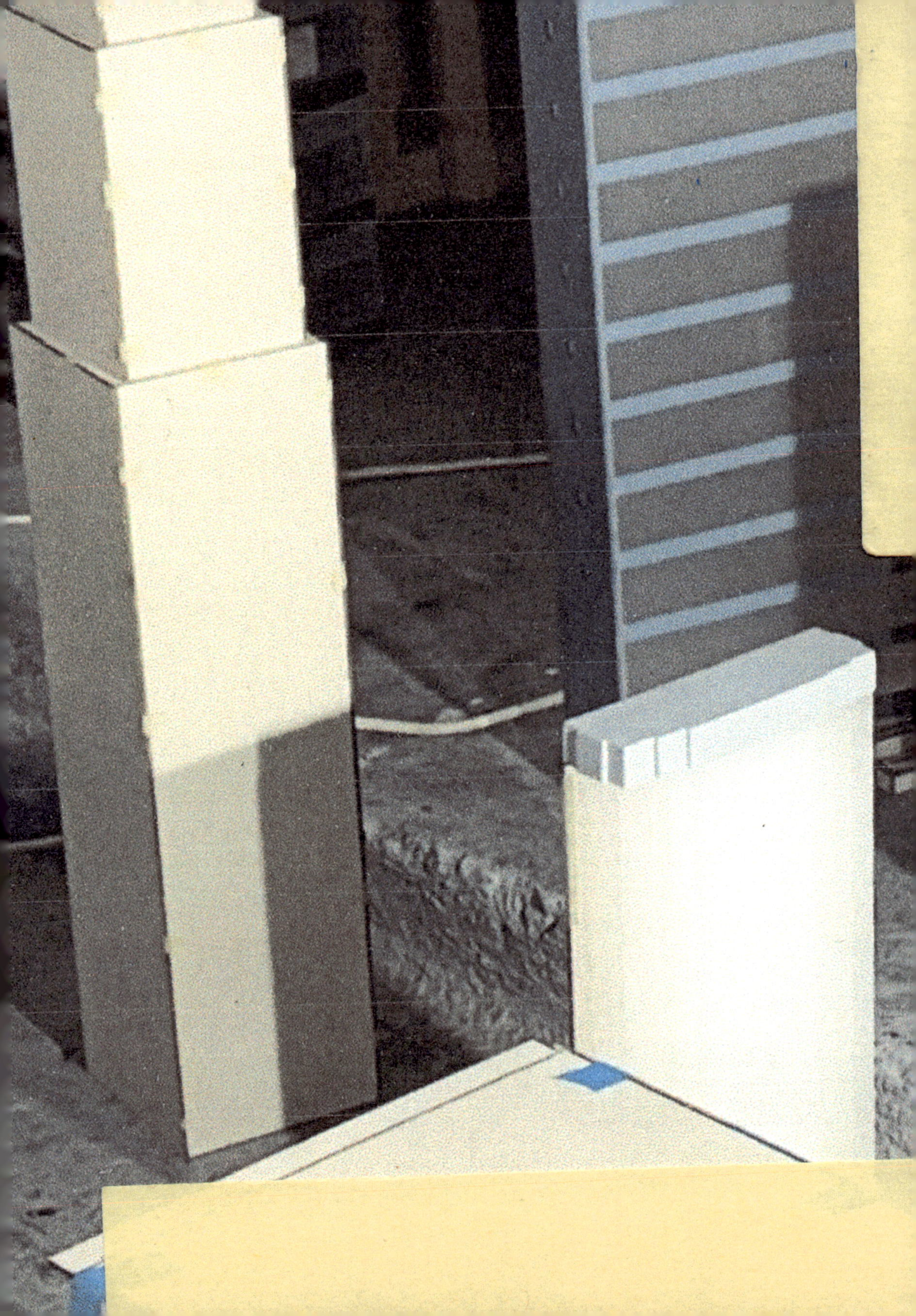

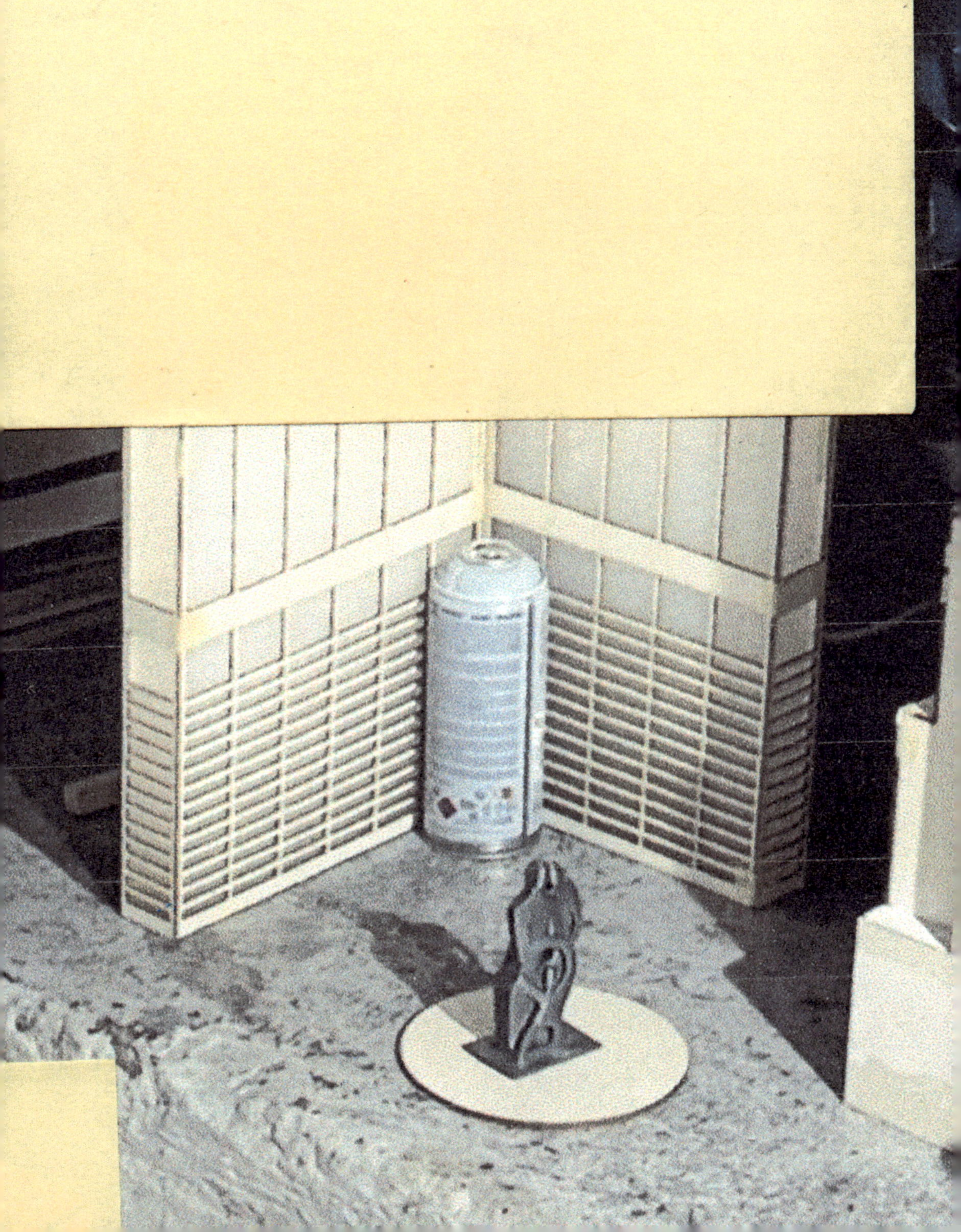

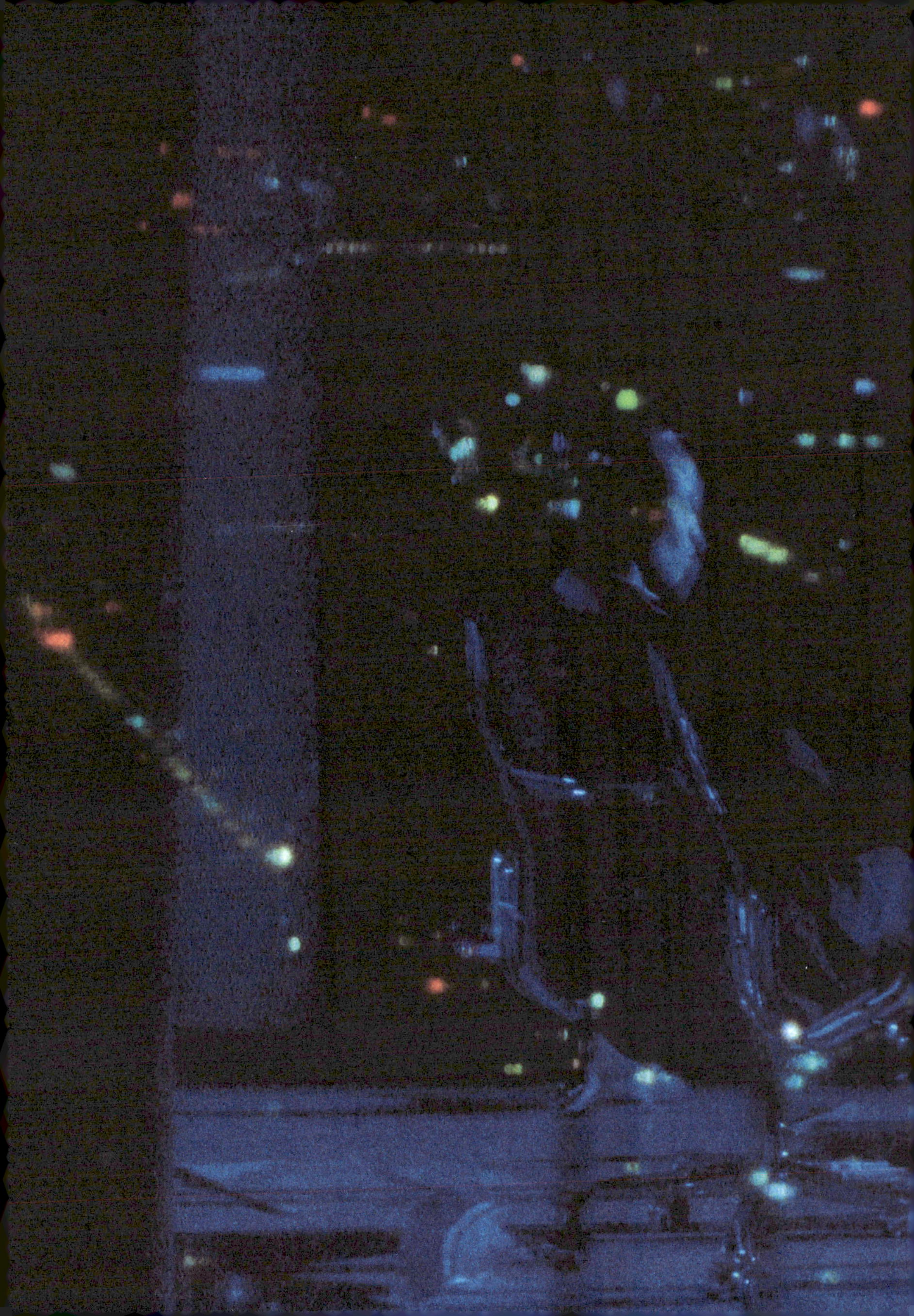

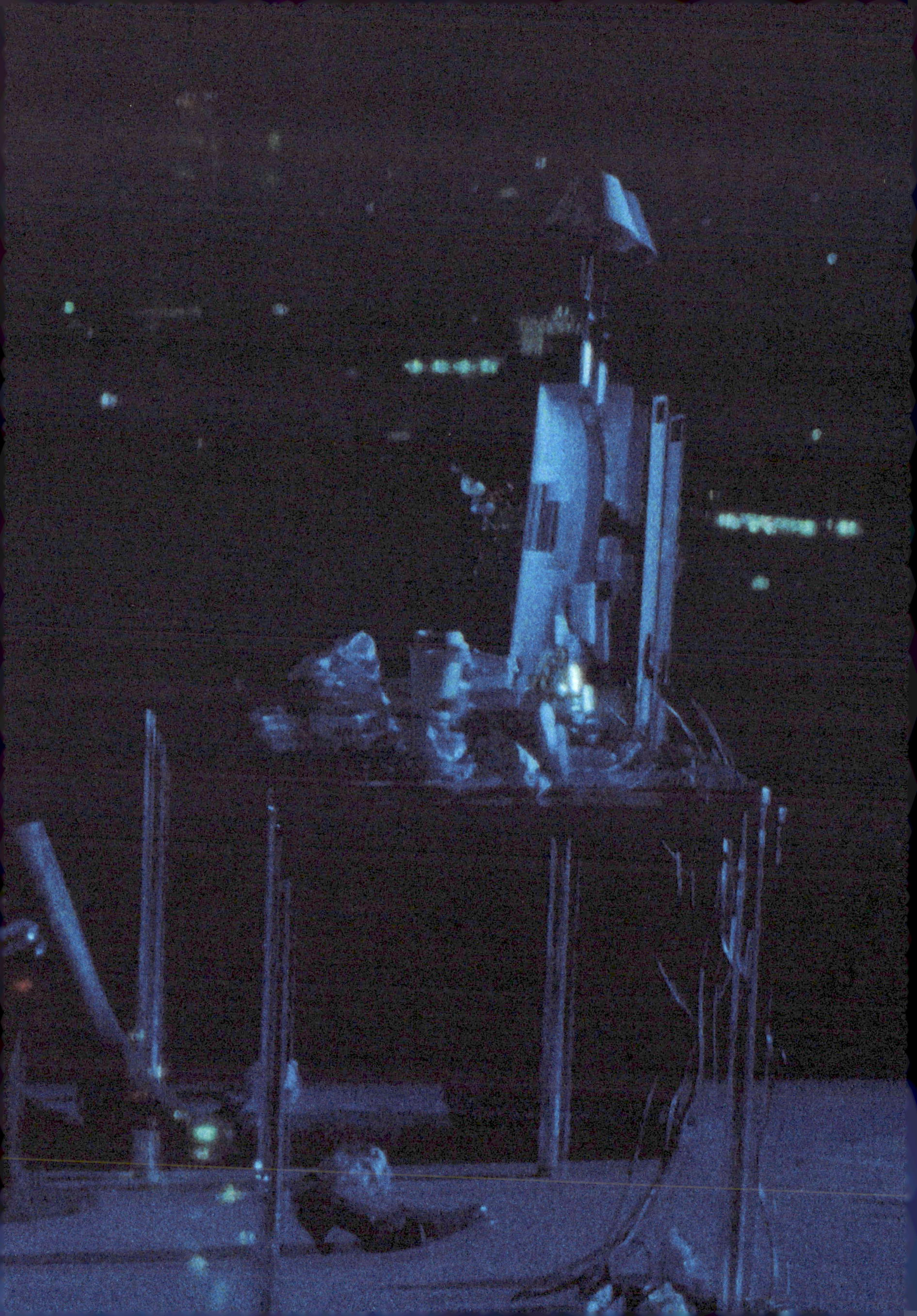

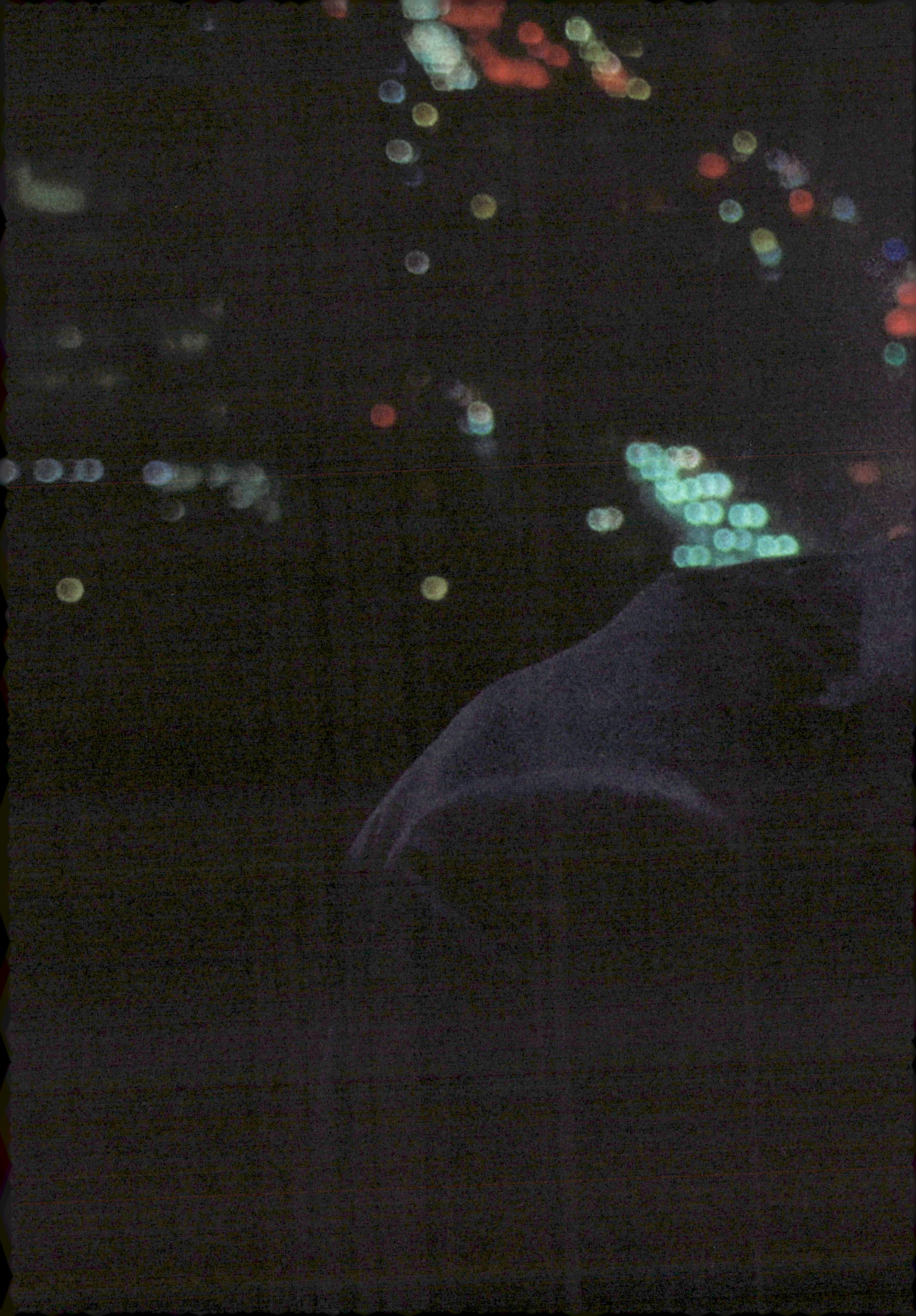

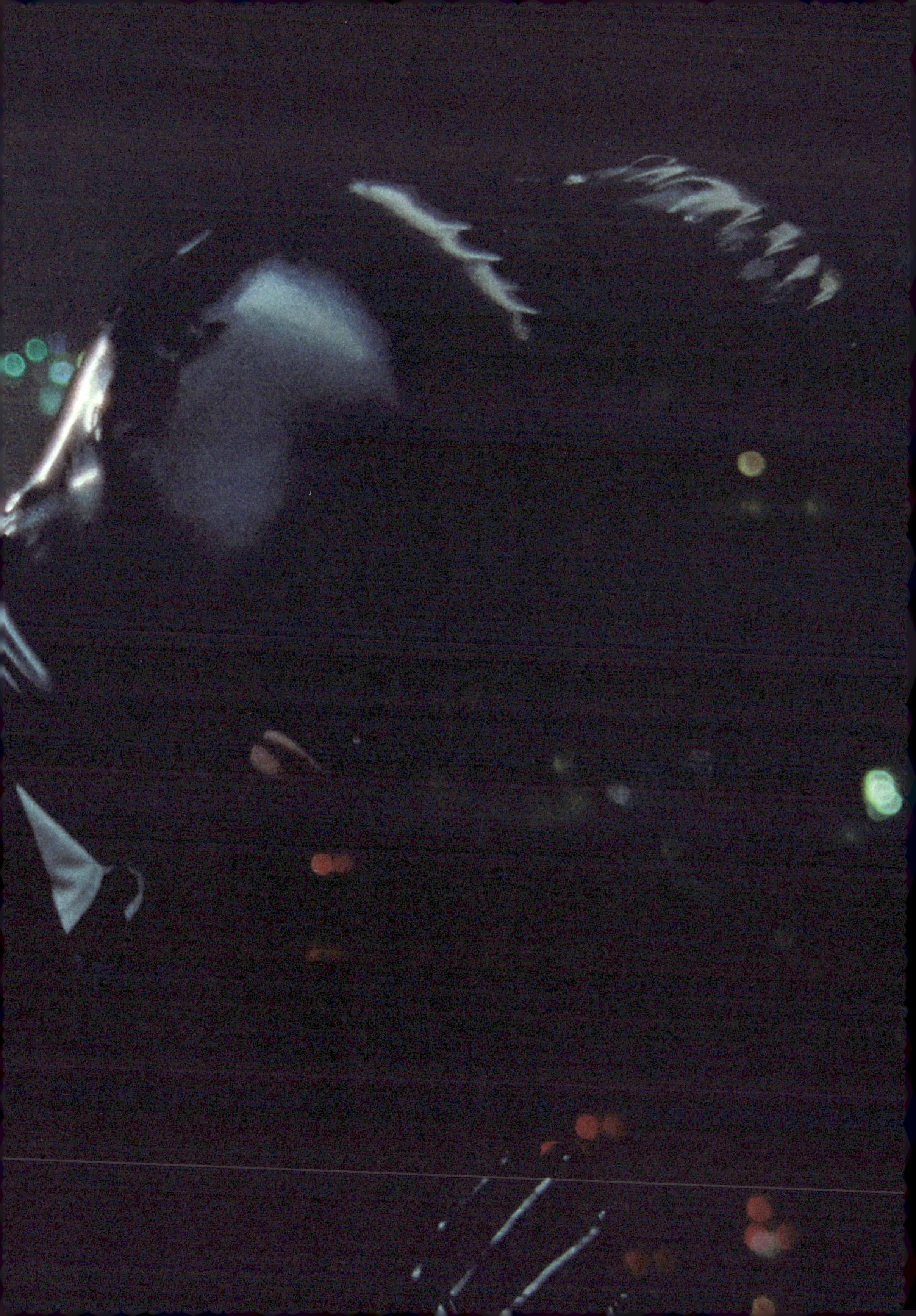

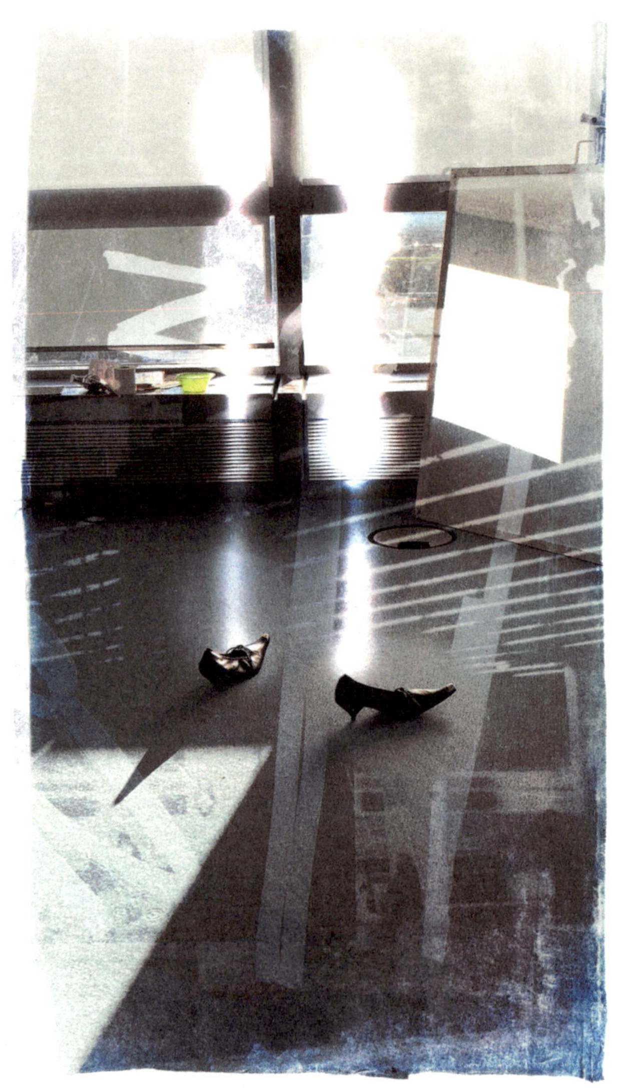

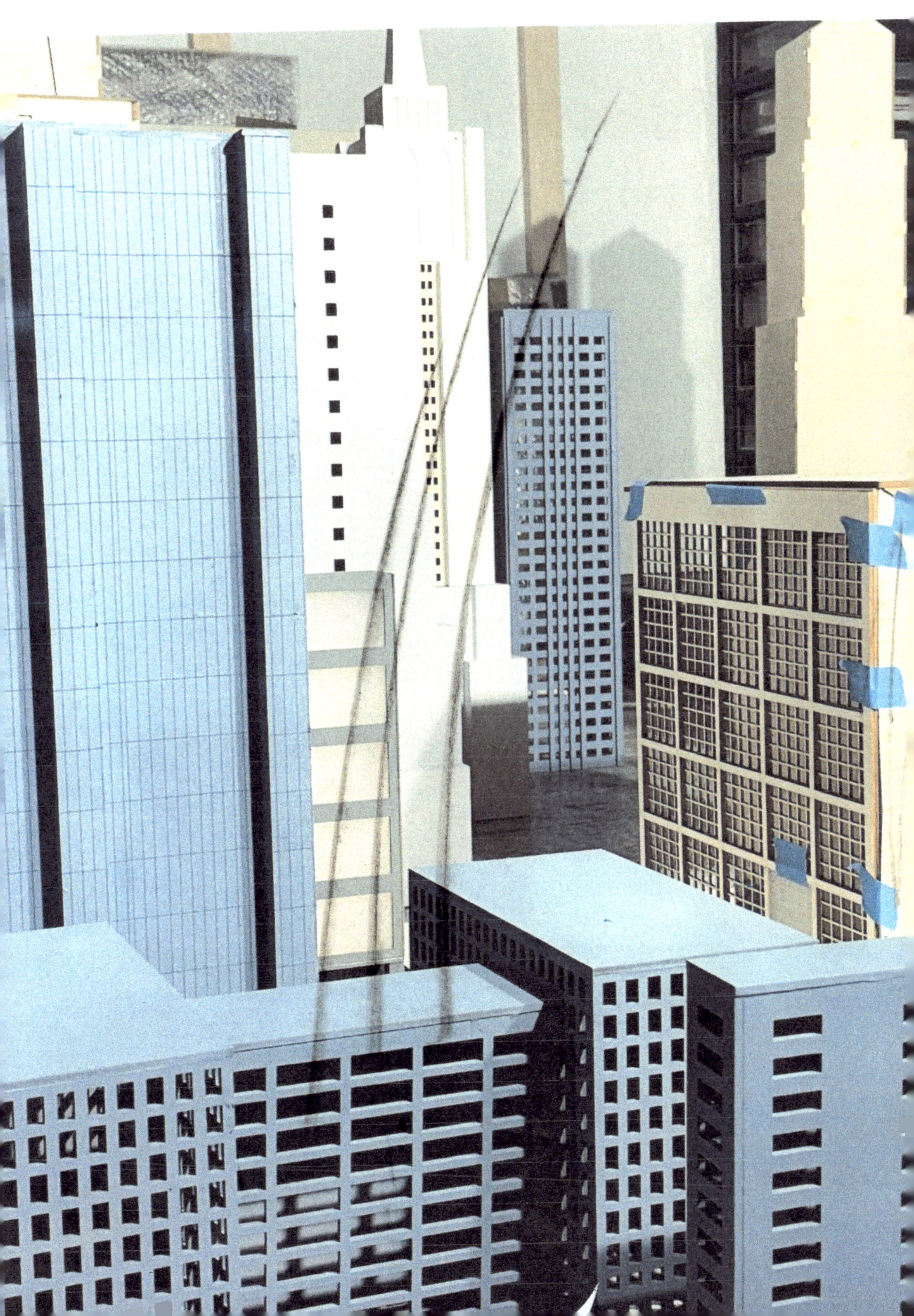

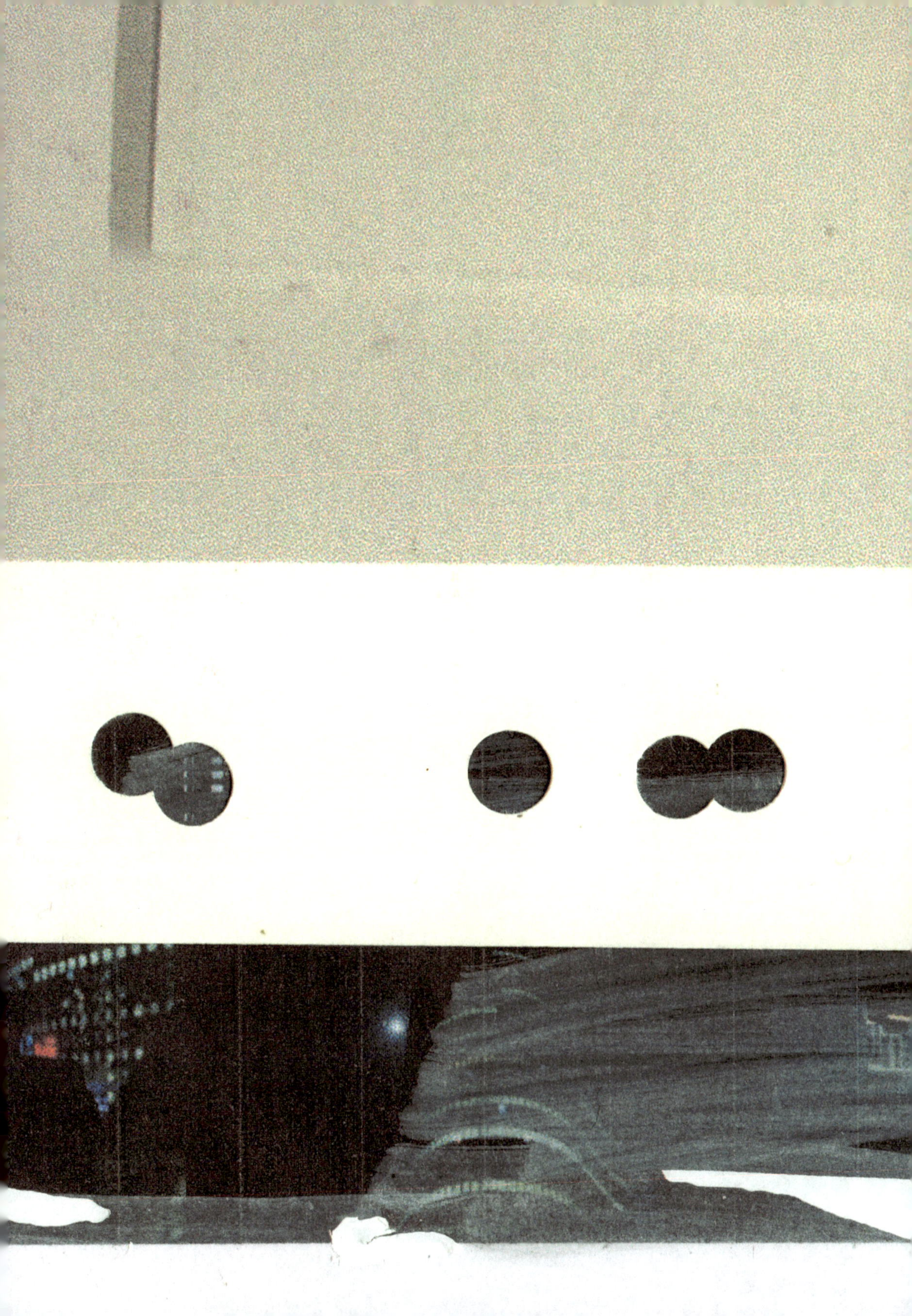

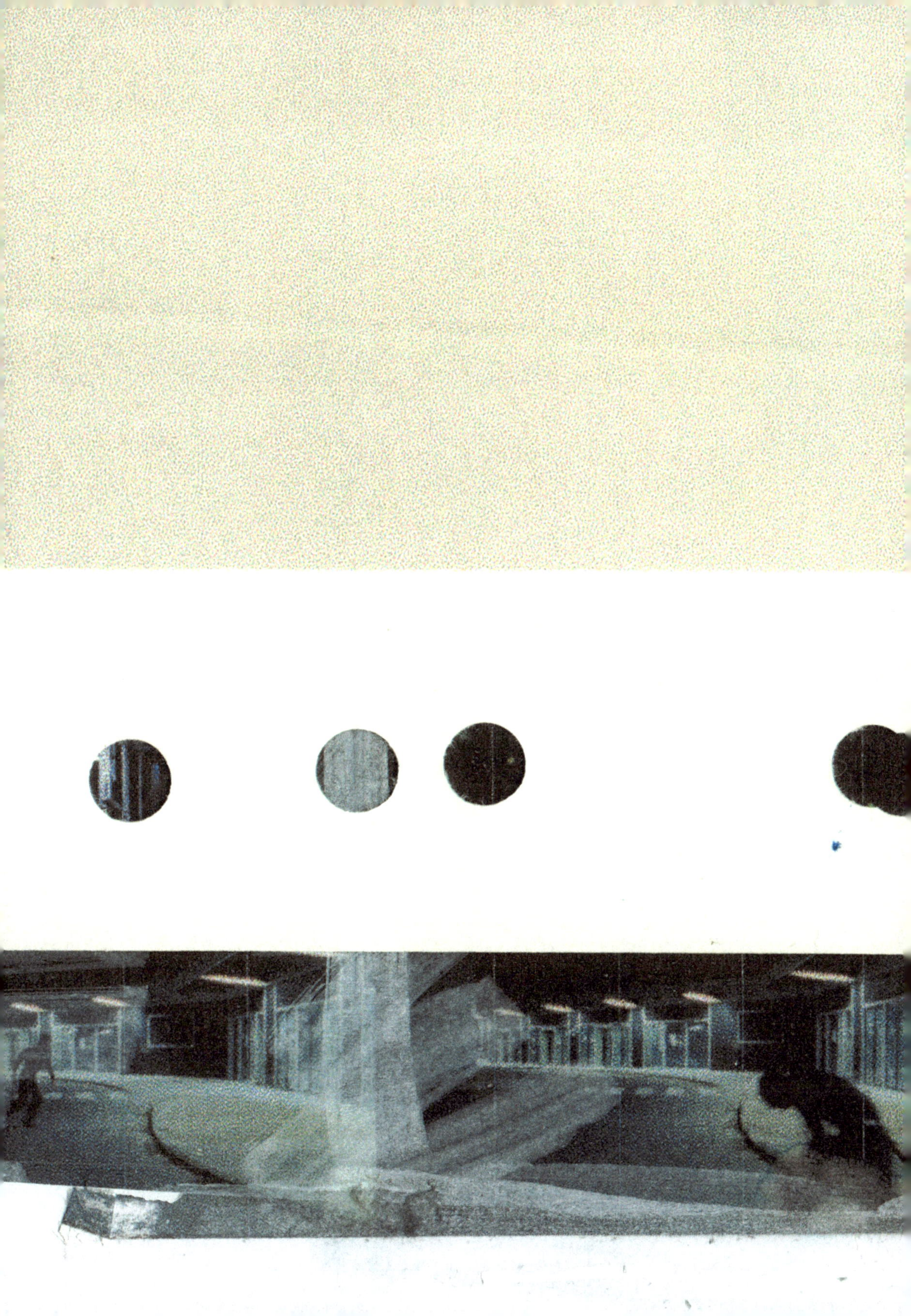

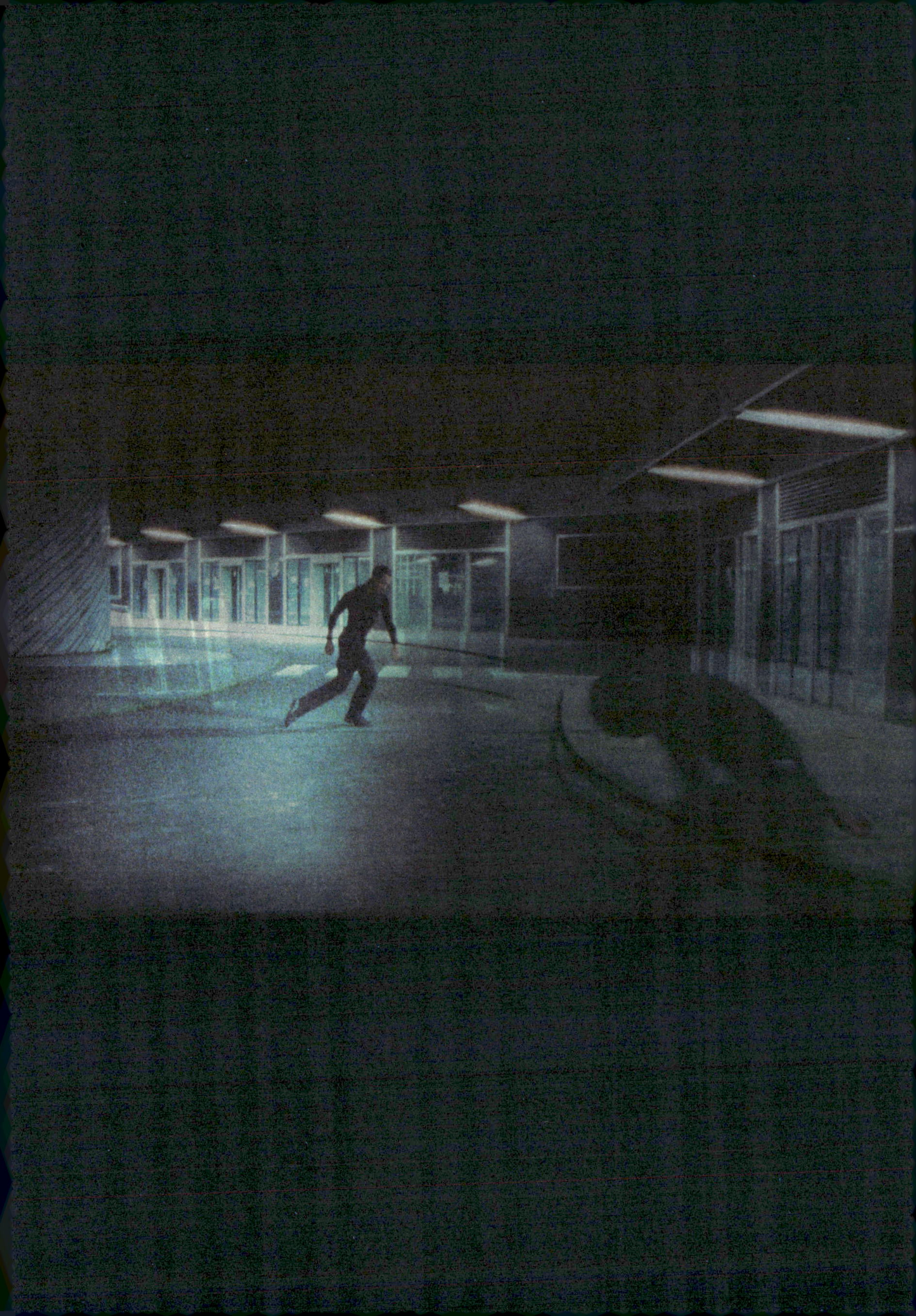

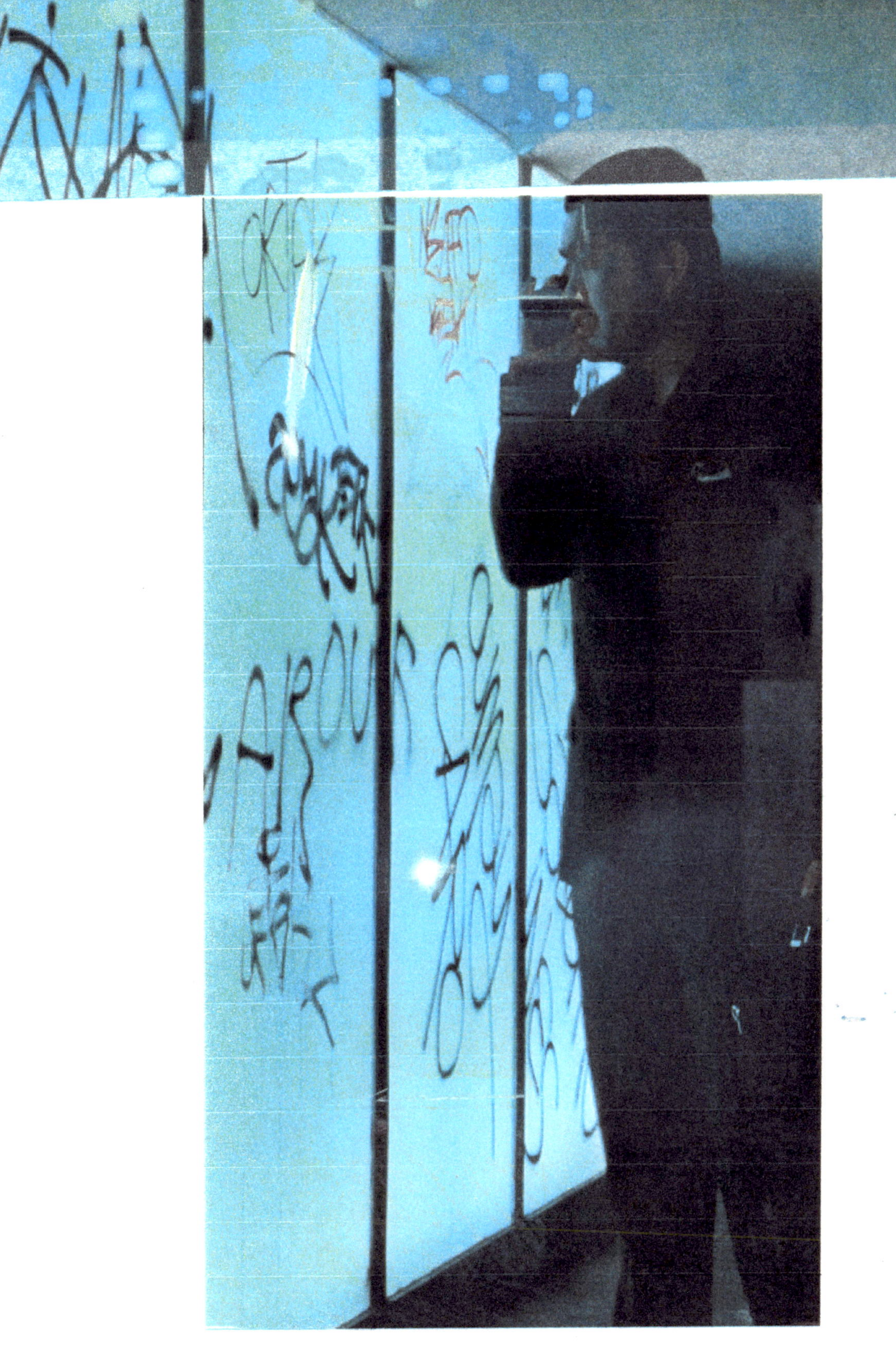

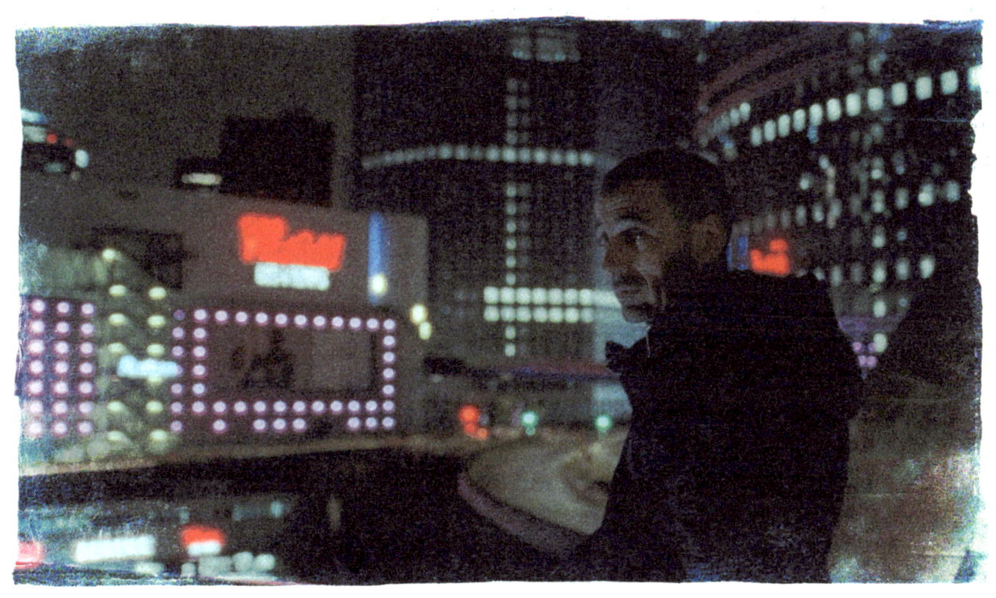

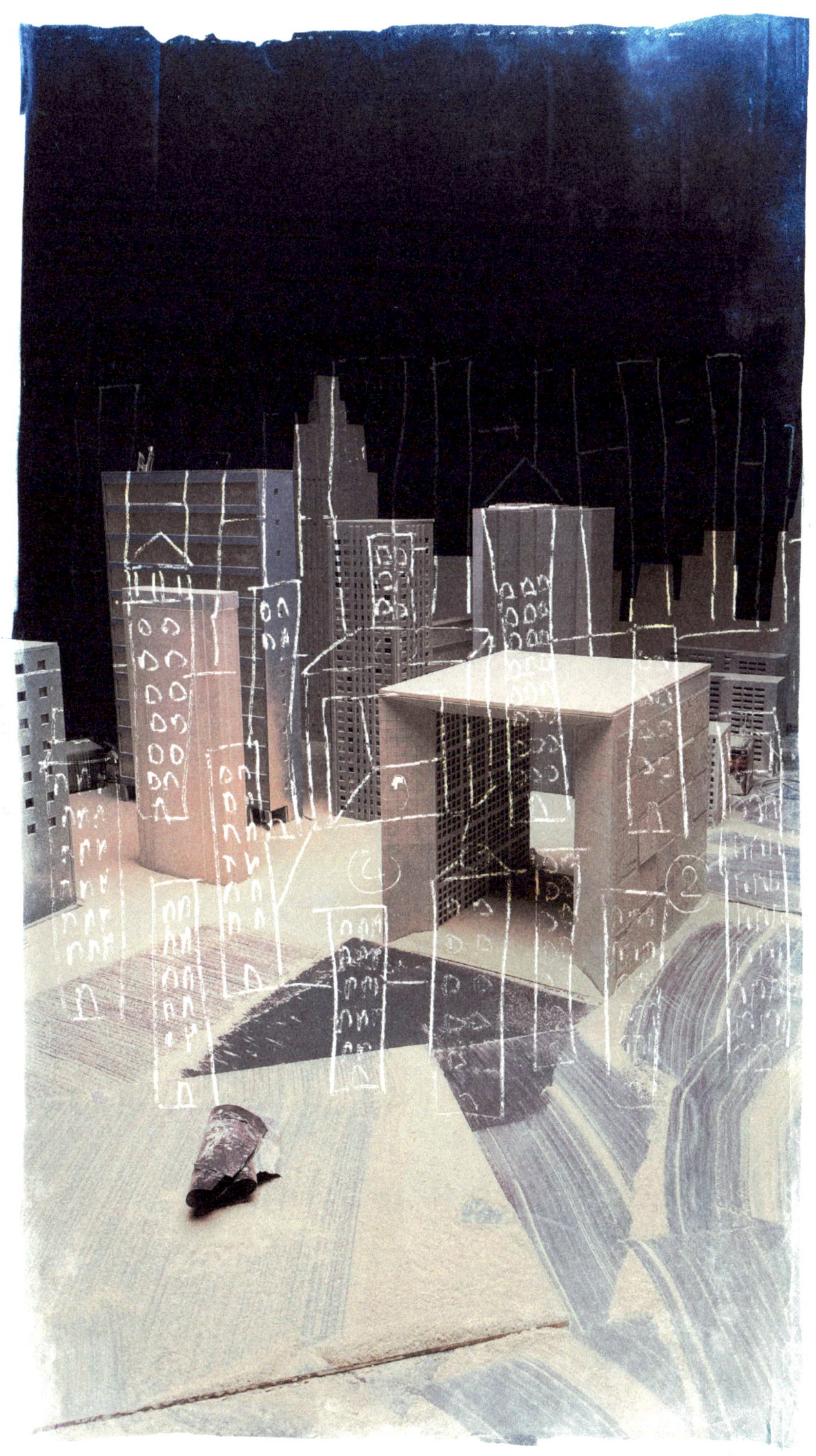

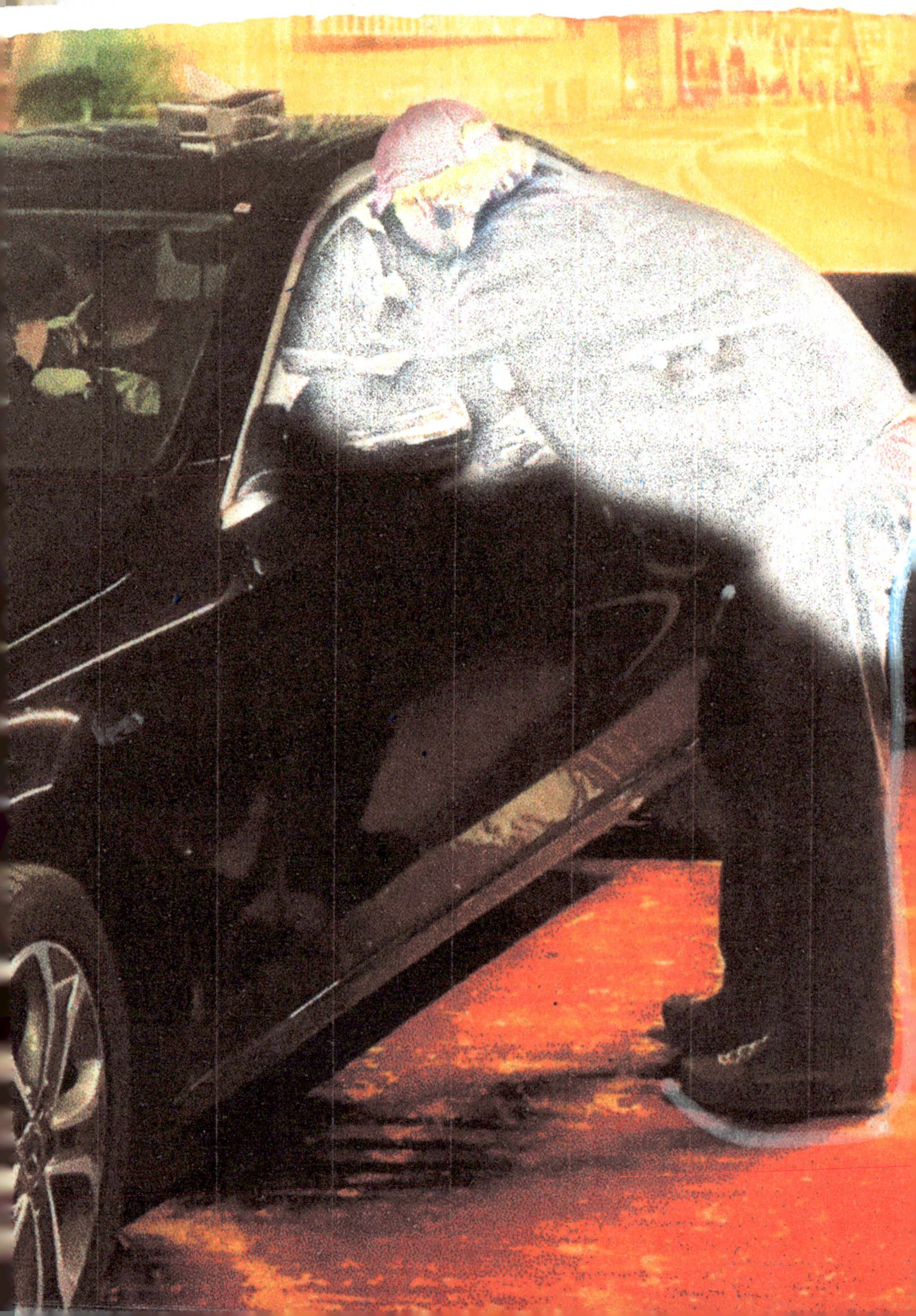

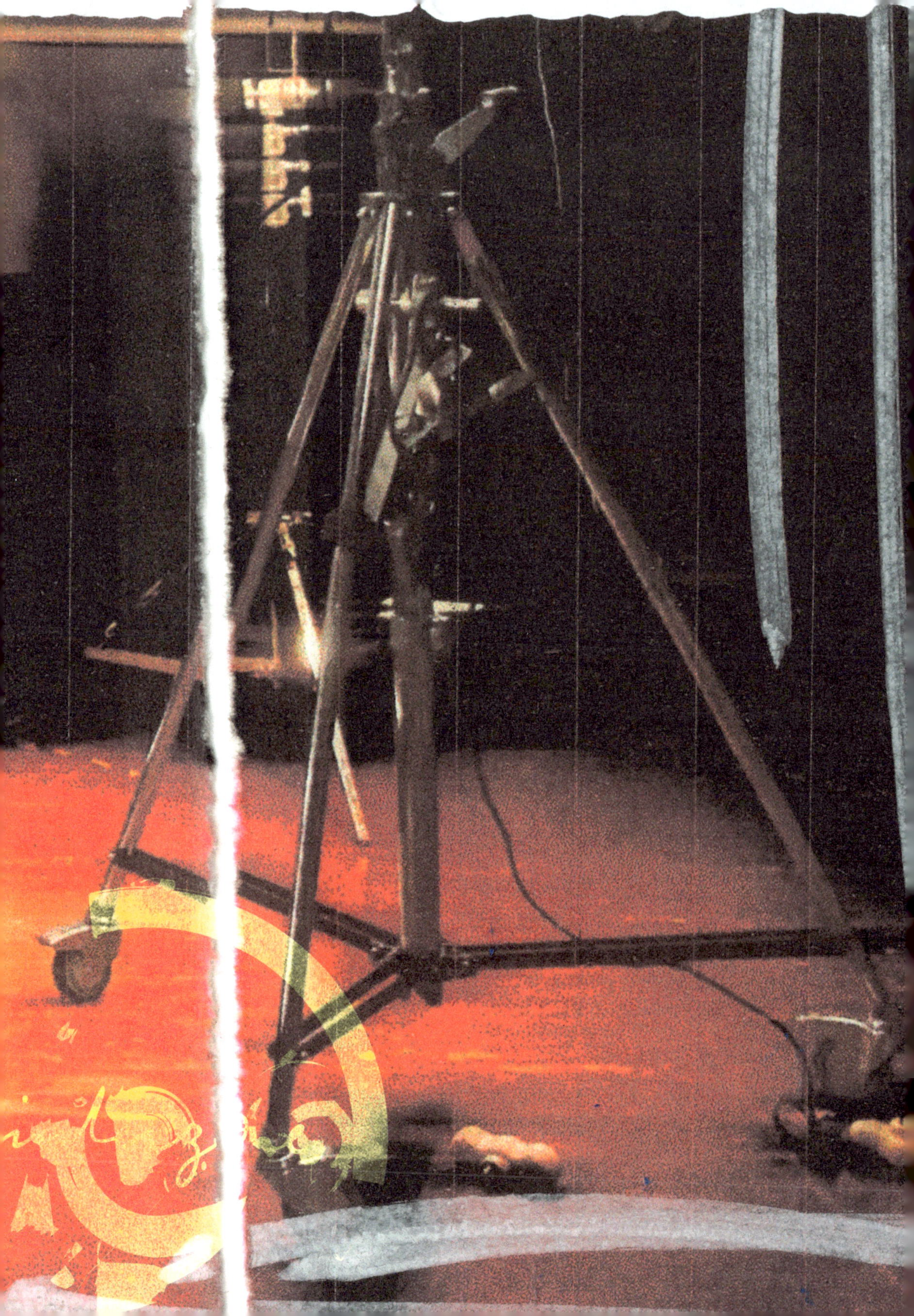

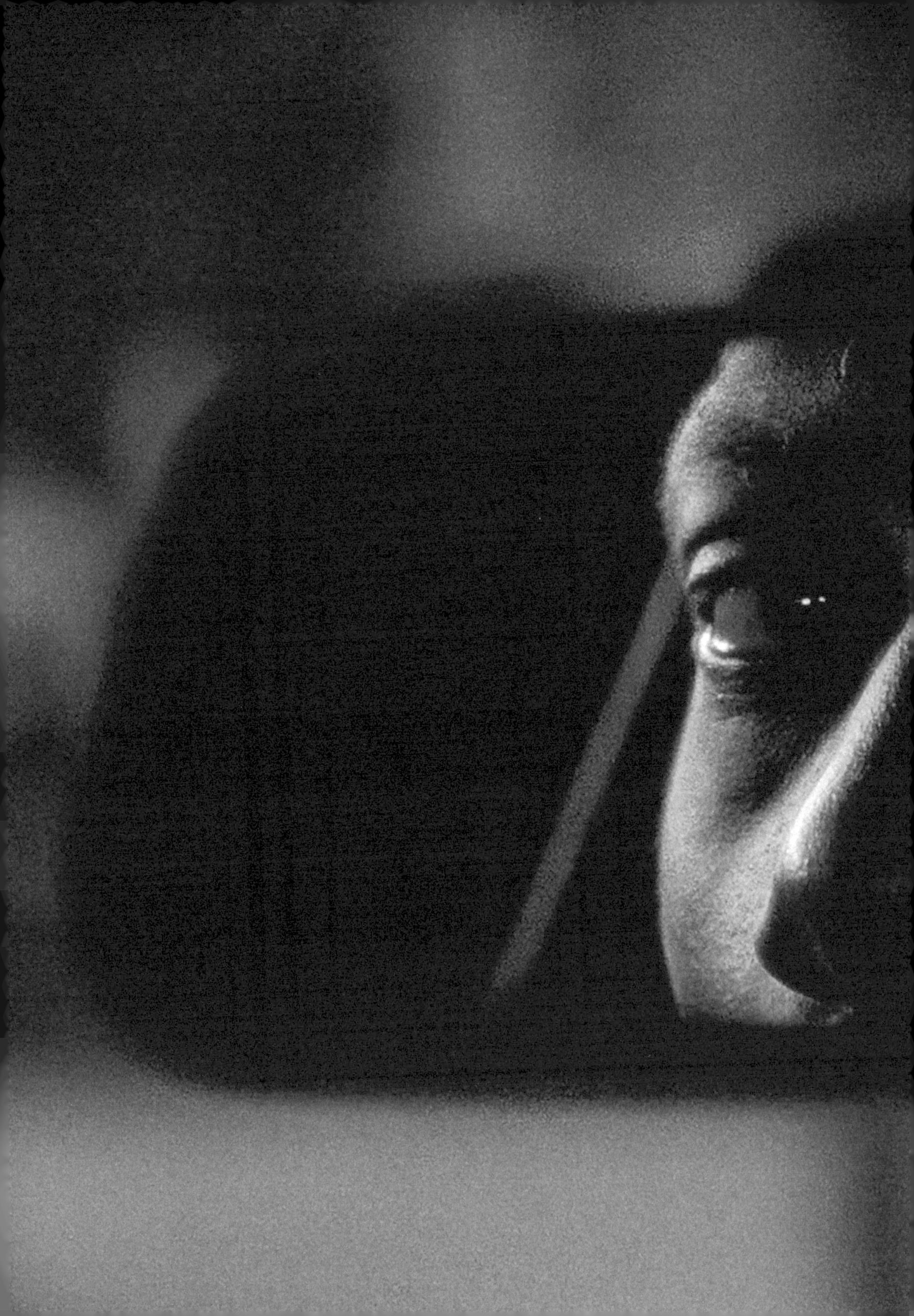

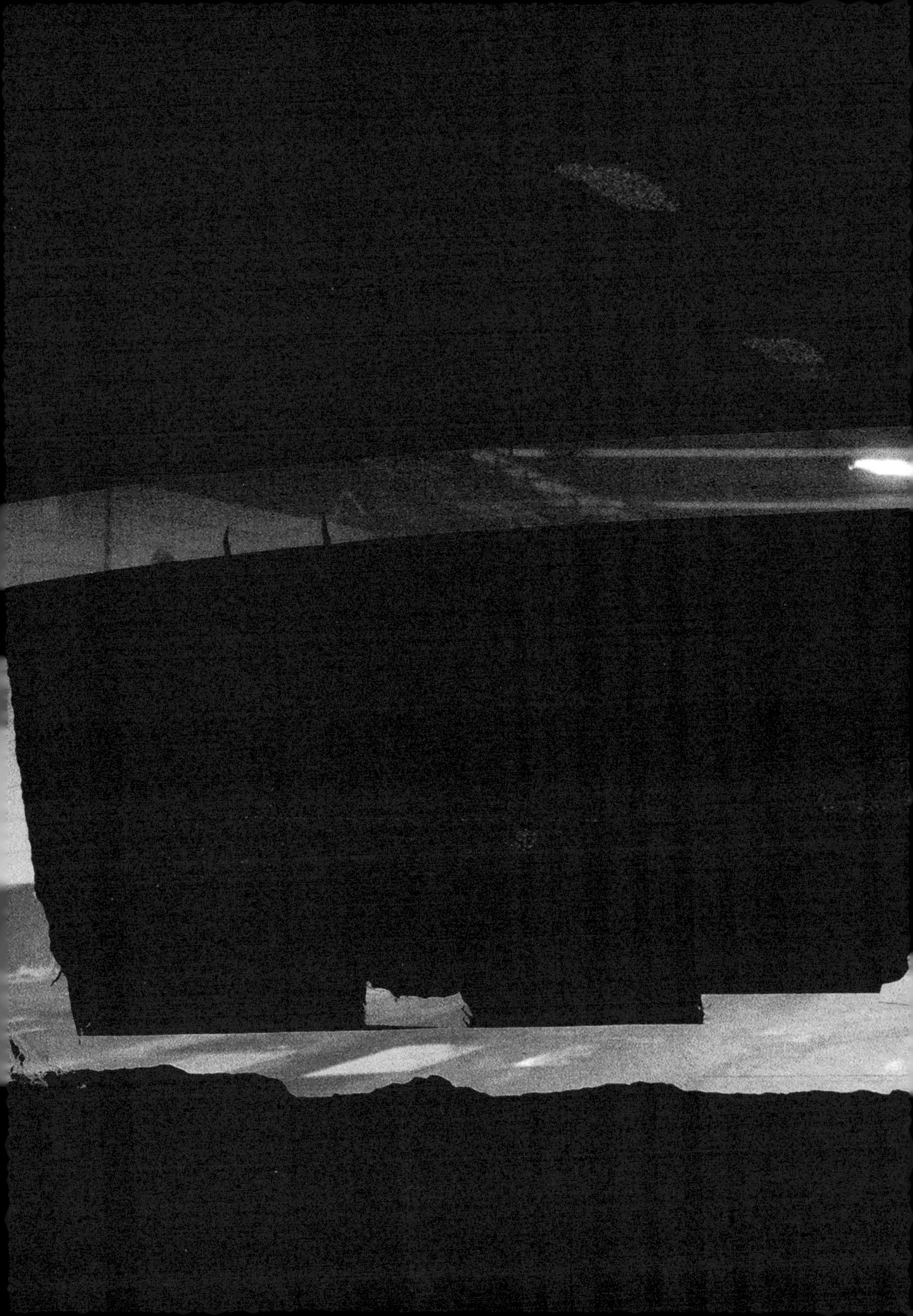

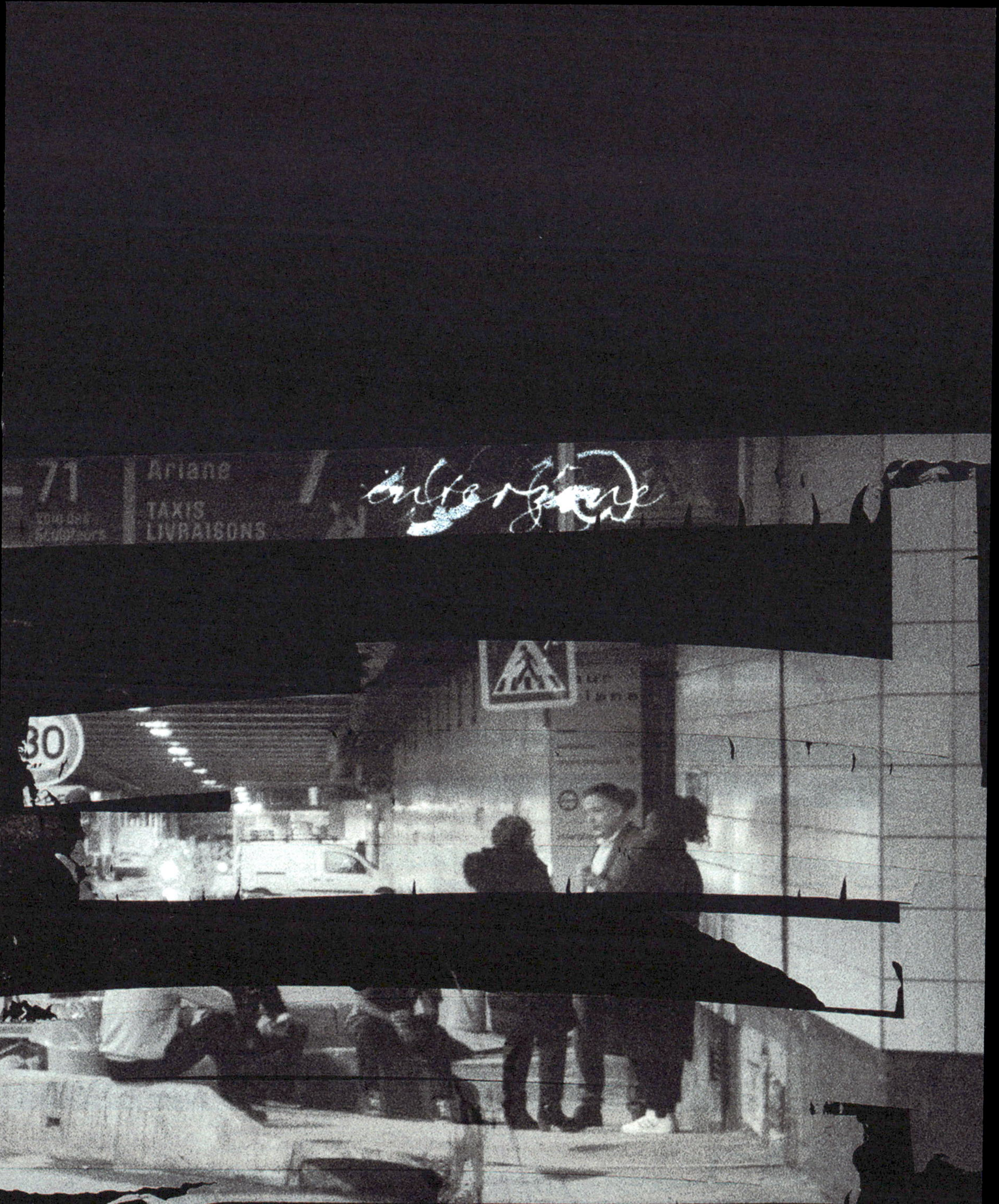

71
Ariane
TAXIS
LIVRAISONS
30

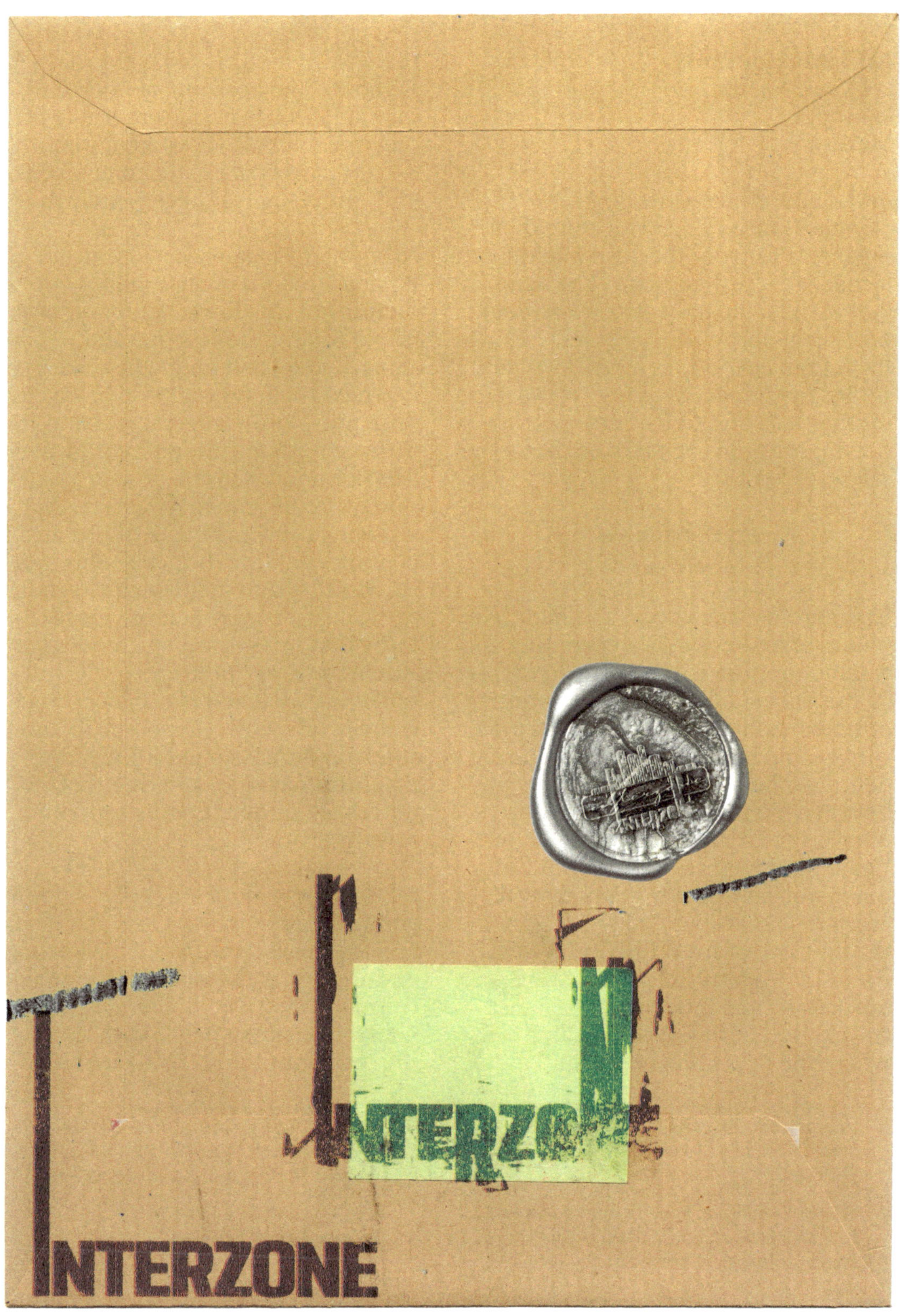

INTERZONE
INTERZONE

All That Remains
Perwana Nazif

Memory

And death is not mine alone. We all die incessantly. The brief time that separates us from the void has the inconsistency of a dream. The dead that we imagine to be far off, we might with a leap throw ourselves less among them than beyond them: this woman, whom I embrace, is dying, and the infinite loss of beings, incessantly flowing, slipping outside of themselves, is ME!

> —Georges Bataille,
> *On Nietzsche*, 1945[1]

Existence between noon and midnight, midnight and noon, is a becoming and waning meridian. There is what feels like an unbearableness, both a suffering of time passing and also time as unsurpassable in the trembling balance delicately held. The blues that occur between them. It is when the day unravels the night's weavings, Walter Benjamin laments, that we hold in our hands, in frailty and upon awakening each morning, "a few fringes of the tapestry of lived life, as loomed for us by forgetting."[2] These fringes are undone and hidden away against the exalted oblivion of midnight, where the beyond is heard (and as the waking hour insists, per Alain Badiou).[3] The horizons of noon and midnight—each on the other side of the other, but also beyond one another—both participate in the remembering and forgetting of these weavings.

All thought is meridian, continues Badiou amid his poetico-philosophical dictums of the diurnal and nocturnal meridian, but it is among these scissions of noon and midnight—the apex in which shadows wane—that memory, sameness, knowledge, truth, and the infinite both appear and withdraw. *Midi* of noon is also a *mi-dit*, a half-said.[4] The psychoanalytic act, that which is the working of these appearances and withdrawals through recognition and misrecognitions of the structures that emerge, necessitates the destitution of knowledge (subjective, of language, of desire) otherwise assumed in a subject. Such is the bereft subject supposed to know, toward an unassumed knowledge[5]—a painful passage, and one that requires (symbolic) deaths unto and toward death.

Of dreams—of melancholy—of (ongoing) catastrophe—of loss and death and the divine. A listing of melancholy endured: it is the mythic noonday demon that strikes medieval Christian men at the sun's apogee with "a proximity so intolerable as to require

---

1. Georges Bataille, *On Nietzsche*, trans. Stuart Kendall (Albany, NY: SUNY Press, 2015), 137.

2. Walter Benjamin, "The Image of Proust," in *Illuminations*, ed. Hannah Arendt, trans. Harry Zohn (New York: Schocken, 1969), 202.

3. Alain Badiou, *Lacan: Anti-Philosophy 3*, trans. Kenneth Reinhard and Susan Spitzer (New York: Columbia University Press, 2018), 9.

4. Badiou, *Lacan*, 20.

5. Badiou, *Lacan*, 26.

camouflage and repression."[6] It is the wreckage of time that the Angelus Novus (Angel of History) faces, piling up, as he is propelled forward everywhere,[7] which is also the ongoing and particularized catastrophe that "*our* ruins had to be personal,"[8] as the anonymous Syrian artist collective Abounaddara has written. It is the eternal in Giovanni da Modena's *The Inferno* (1410) lit up by Dante's "flies of fire" (fireflies) that forever feebly burn.[9] It is the blue eyeshadow that repeats and recurs in *The Death of Maria Malibran* (1972) amid formal displacement and repetition. Lost in space, but not time, it is the constant passage to awaiting cosmologies of Valentin Noujaïm's *The Blue Star* (2020), where blue cities sit among blue ancient ruins on a blue star to come, anticipating and encountering the perpetual and impossible arrival by the brown man escaping what forces determine and fix him. It is Sufi mystic Ibn Arabi's injunction that "the time of a thing is its presence, but I am out of time and You are out of time, so I am Your time and You are my time. I am Your presence and You are my presence" where the existence of the world has neither duration nor extension.[10]

Our mythologies and narratives tell not of a foreclosure of the world at the site of irreconcilable agony, but rather of an appearance, an opening, a moment of production from other times and also outside of time, or an anticipation of what is yet to come that watches over the end. For melancholy is a flexible signifier. Between a future and none sits this precarity of the *chance* of an inscription after an end.[11] It guides a writing or an image that may already be—as in the emoji-inflected comments of an online group gathered to reminisce about a nightclub that no longer exists, presented in *Pacific Club* (2022), the first film in Noujaïm's trilogy *La Défense*—or that will take place, both re-signified and experienced, but also delayed and simultaneously effaced.

6. Giorgio Agamben, *Stanzas: Word and Phantasm in Western Culture*, trans. Ronald L. Martinez (Minneapolis: University of Minnesota Press, 1993), 5.

7. Walter Benjamin, "Theses on the Philosophy of History," in *Illuminations*, 257.

8. Abounaddara, "Waiting for Resurrection," in *Abounaddara: The Ruins We Carry* (Berkeley: Berkeley Art Museum and Pacific Film Archive, 2024), 10.

9. Georges Didi-Huberman, *Survival of the Fireflies* (Minneapolis: University of Minnesota Press, 2018), 1–2.

10. Muhammad ʿAlī Hājj Yūsuf, *Ibn ʿArabī: Time and Cosmology* (London: Routledge, 2008), 57.

11. David L. Eng and David Kazanjian, "Introduction: Mourning Remains," in *Loss: The Politics of Mourning*, ed. David Kazanjian and David L. Eng (Berkeley: University of California Press, 2002), 5.

Dream

The sequence of the volumes of
La Défense are as follows:

1. Memory

2. Dream (*Father, can't you see that
I am burning?*[12])

3. Death

Ruptures of experience and witnessing, history and truth, emerge across
the sacred, melancholic images of
Noujaïm's works. *What remains in
what is lost?* ask these images of
loss which are at the same time lost

images. The question negotiates the
legible and the illegible in itself, which
encompasses the illegibility of the
legible-as-remains. Accordingly, such
is the negotiation of aesthetics in
Noujaïm's practice around the unimaginable and the "un-image-able."[13]
Images become named as ghost stills
in Noujaïm's *Ghost Still* series (2025),
silkscreens printed on the material
used for production and historical
"progression" and "modernization"
(raw steel, in this instance). The extraction, abstraction, and disposability
of materials correspond to the physical
and psychic extraction, abstraction,
and disposability of certain bodies
(recall that "our ruins had to be personal"). A wreckage piles up behind
the Angelus Novus that it eternally
confronts, where figures in motion are
materially fixed and imprinted in and
onto oblivion.

In philosopher and literary critic Marc
Nichanian's "Catastrophic Mourning,"
he writes through Armenian author
Zabel Essayan's writings as bearing
witness to the experience of the Armenian genocide. The genocide, Nichanian
argues, should be named and thought
through as the Catastrophe precisely
because of the interdiction of mourning. Named as the Catastrophe, it resists
a claim of representation of an event
in totality, in positivist terms, which,
thus, reproduces a calculable logic of
the means and end(s) of genocide.[14]
Essayan's writing, on the other hand,
does "other than prove the historical

---

12. Jacques Lacan notoriously recounts an
episode from Sigmund Freud where a
father sleeps next to the room in which
his dead son lies. The father dreams of the
son speaking to him and taking his arm,
admonishing, "Father, can't you see that
I am burning?" The father awakens to see
the candles by the dead son aflame on the
bed in which he lies, flames threatening to
devour the corpse, and the man supposedly
watching guard over the dead son fast
asleep. The dream is the (missed) encounter
with the Real. It is not just that fragments
of reality make their way into dreams less
than dreams entering into reality—where
upon waking, the father sees his dream
in waking life and that the one meant to
watch over the dead son is asleep and thus
remains dreaming—but, importantly, it is
the bed, the marker of both dreams and, in
the case of the corpse, death, that is aflame.
The boundary between dream and waking
reality, death and sleep, burns up—an
operation at play in Noujaïm's *To Exist
Under Permanent Suspicion* (2024). Jacques
Lacan, *The Four Fundamental Concepts of
Psychoanalysis*, ed. Jacques-Alain Miller,
trans. Alan Sheridan (New York: Norton,
1978), 58.

---

13. Marc Nichanian, "Catastrophic Mourning,"
in *Loss*, 111.

14. Eng and Kazanjian, "Introduction:
Mourning Remains," 9.

truth of near-total annihilation." Here, one is "obliged to do something other than chronicle murdered bodies, pain, and death" in the face of the *total* event, where an ethnicity was partly sacrificed, its blood was spilled, so that ethnicity would disappear as a principle in the concept and in the action of the state, what one calls the struggle for freedom, which is then no longer a particular freedom, but indeed a universal freedom, that of the citizen, a freedom in relation to and in opposition with ethnic belonging.[15]

This universal freedom disperses the total event into obscurity in effacing its historical and material specificity through a declared opposition to ethnic belonging, which is presented as threatening to the universalized citizen-subject. The diffused ongoing-ness of the event in the lived experiences of those sacrificed to the state's violences (in the enforced attachment to ethnic belonging, for example, as violently produced difference in order to eradicate difference) further plunges into obscurity. State-weaponized dispersion and diffusion is a thread picked up in much of Noujaïm's practice, unspooled in the examination of its specified plaits and larger frames to world, to subject, to fantasy, and the imaginary.

This specific dispersion and diffusion produces and maintains supposed universal freedom and the citizen-subject. Meaning, for "universal freedom" to exist, it will always reproduce the circumscription of itself to mark an outside—with such

circumscription also, simultaneously, as its condition of existence. This outside is created through either the Catastrophe of "remainderless extinction" or remaindered as varied violences of the ongoing catastrophes across empire- and subject-as-citizen-making, both of which it strategically disavows or "remembers."[16] It is this "something other than" chronicling that Nichanian, through Essayan, urges. A "something other than" is an other scene, bearing witness to "the between perception and consciousness" which is also dreamwork,[17] which is also an intermediate realm of existence. It is this space of "something other than"—in face of, and in recognition that, representation exceeds the possibility of "bodies, pain, and death" and, more precisely, their afterlives—that Noujaïm locates in his work while also surfacing the constructions and boundary-making of universal freedom and its citizen-subjects.

Noujaïm's films are not created *ex nihilo*, nor are they an unmasking. They are rather a rewriting of the unknown in relation to an address toward visions of the soul, of the metaphysical dimension of the unknown—without making it known. In art's role as revealer (in the sense of baring so as to re-veil) of the withdrawn, where memory is not limited to human re-memory nor archived

---

16. Essayan thinks through "remainderless extinction" as "sacrifice." Nichanian, "Catastrophic Mourning," 108–09.

17. Lacan, *The Four Fundamental Concepts of Psychoanalysis*, 56.

---

15. Nichanian, "Catastrophic Mourning," 107.

images,[18] which necessarily involves the technological, political, ethical, and, certainly, juridical, Noujaïm attempts to trace the breaching and inscription of forces historical and otherwise (symbolic, libidinal). This tracing necessarily implicates the forces' deferral and repetition, which is not recognizable as repetition. Like dreamwork, this traced breach is a way of thinking distinct from the thinking of consciousness and the worlds it inhabits and propagates, including the shared reality of everyday life in the aftermath of varied and ongoing catastrophes. Dreamwork is beyond representation, identification, and, perhaps, witness. Rather, it bears a different witnessing, a different image and perception—much as Noujaïm's work demands. Such is the constant arrival to a missed encounter, an aporia, here again, of what is both unimaginable and un-image-able,[19] specific to not only desire, but also the particulars of the "sacrificed" and the generations that follow, in the face of ongoing and varied catastrophes.

Melancholia littered the holy site of *PANTHEON*, Noujaïm's 2025 exhibition at Kunsthalle Basel: monstrous monuments of protection, psychic and more, reduced to concrete debris, ghosts of aegis, against a very material emergent scaffolding. Throats (of the *Gargoyles*, 2025) were laid bare to sacrifice. A structure materialized, coming forth from under the remains of a sacrifice. Not a burial, but a

resurrection toward the withdrawn.[20] But it is also the surfacing of protection for the ultimate defense materialized in the French business district La Défense. A truly grotesque construction of so-called universal freedom and the subjects it both relies on and cataclysmically reproduces, La Défense is the site of a moving image in threes, which are but again deferrals and repetitions, which repeat not the same. *To Exist Under Permanent Suspicion* (2024), as an endless repetition of catastrophes where particular bodies are constantly exposed as suspicious and dangerous to this universal freedom, burns it all down at the end of the film in its fantastical conclusion. All that remains, in this dream, are ashes.

Death

Among these monuments of the *Pantheon*, which include a meridian that involves not merely two sides as an either/or, but also the constitutive in-between, as well as a sequence that upsets an order in endless repetition, lies a map of the crossroads of the Fates. A trinity of past, present, future—an order of things—undone. To follow the map is to trace, efface, and retrace a frayed thread of destiny in its perpetual unraveling. This map images a politics and an aesthetics of territorialization and spatial displacement that does not seek to resolve

---

18. Jalal Toufic, *The Withdrawal of Tradition Past a Surpassing Disaster* (Forthcoming Books, 2009), 54, 61.

19. Nichanian, "Catastrophic Mourning," 111.

20. This is the "attempt to resurrect what has become withdrawn due to a surpassing disaster." Toufic, *The Withdrawal of Tradition Past a Surpassing Disaster*, 19.

the universal and the particular. It specifies the ambiguous cohesion that occurs within improvised undertakings in the face of vulnerability and melancholia that both exposes and evades the mechanisms of state regulation and control of bodies that "materialize a political world of social appropriations."[21]

In "Tacit Alliances, Not Knowing Togetherness" (2025), urban studies scholars Michele Lancione and AbdouMaliq Simone write of densely populated districts in Delhi, Mexico City, Lagos, and elsewhere, where informal relations, "mundane alliances," encounters, and positions take place as the "unspecified" and indeterminable outcomes of these urban densities colliding and acting upon one another—without romanticizing the improvisations, opacities, and endurances necessary in face of material, political, and symbolic precarity, disposability, regulation, and extraction.[22] And yet, there is something else in these ongoing remakings that is beyond survival, becoming "that which is lived for." These circulations of "pirates, cartels, hustlers, brokers, mercenaries, traders, priests, fabricators, casual labour, 'advisors,' [and] tricksters extend the operations of molar organizations," or instituted

organizations (as in bounded, representable, or legible as such), with topologically open, "strange" collaborations that include the immaterial and the transcendent.

Such collaborations include after-midnight conversations about death among skyscraper guards and cleaning staff, which also implicates the ghosts that haunt the skyscrapers as seen (and unseen) in Noujaïm's *Demons to Diamonds* (2025). These ongoing negotiations of the "more ephemeral forms of collective life," open to the inexplicable and the unspecified, the unknown and the never-have-been, cannot exclude "the multitude of ghosts—lives for whom there is yet to be justice."[23] The collaborations neither formalize themselves nor yield something discernible, including the "ghosts" themselves, but a force is exerted, one that is disquieting and unsettling. Under the steel and glass landscapes of *Demons to Diamonds*, a cursed Denis Lavant cannot free the wires from which he is entangled, like the snarls and entwinings of these collaborations that extend to dimensions beyond horizontality and verticality. He does not pull the strings in which he is held, but he can exert pressure on them, inducing rifts, as he narrativizes.

These ghosts, and these "tacit proximities,"[24] including the ghosts of tacit proximities across not just time, but space (the ever-expansive monstrosity of the territorialization

---

21. Eng and Kazanjian, "Introduction: Mourning Remains," 11.

22. This is a competing opacity against state mechanisms that are also cloaked in opacity so as to escape (re)cognition toward endless reproduction. Michele Lancione and AbdouMaliq Simone, "Tacit Alliances: Not Knowing Togetherness," *Explorations in Space and Society*, no. 70 (March 2025): 10.

23. Lancione and Simone, "Tacit Alliances," 12, 10.

24. Lancione and Simone, "Tacit Alliances," 12.

and universalization of Western liberalism that terrorizes again and again), haunt Noujaïm's films in form and persistence, but also in the materialization of the invisible, the withdrawn.[25] Ghosts are the subject of his films (*Ghost Still* returns) without speaking for the dead.[26]

These open and mobile circulations of exchange in the making of alliances that do not yet—or, perhaps, ever—"know" their togetherness do not, as Lancione and Simone write, assemble within a grammar of the revolutionary left, and yet they may "provide for multitudes of revolutionary intent."[27] Here, then, it is the persistence of the unconscious, rather than consciousness, in the making of a political subject (new forms of subjectivity, subject formations, collective meanings). These mundane alliances in face of contractive and boundaried spaces of autonomy in the city, among lives made vulnerable and disposable, are not necessarily toward revolutionary yields, nor new subject formations, even if they provide for its multitudes, even as they are not passive. It is as Nichanian argues against reading Essayan's monument of mourning,

or witness to the Catastrophe, as a "political response." That is, unless we believe that when Antigone buries her brother Polynices against her uncle King Creon's decree to neither bury nor mourn him, "she is already, or once again, carrying out a political duty."[28]

Such alliances, compressed and knotty, are not easily decided as "virtuous or destructive," let alone named and met as political resistance. These dense weavings of causality, reciprocity, and exchange, points of ongoing coming-aparts and coming-togethers, express a general orientation or gesture that is more and more open to distortion, mutation, and improvisation.[29] It is a "withdrawal from distinction," indifferent and indirect.[30] For these informal solidarities, far more implicated within gestures than discourses or ideologies or even identifications, evade established systems of political discourse just as they evade institutionalizing themselves. Such elusion does not bear witness, depending on whose ulterior and anterior gaze, and obfuscates political recognition, even if this is eventually not the case. Its articulation is not one of coherence and legibility, for that legibility, its formalization, its name, would be all that remains.[31]

---

25. Toufic, *The Withdrawal of Tradition Past a Surpassing Disaster*, 57.

26. "But precisely none of these authors would claim to be the emissary of the dead; they are aware how indecent it is to talk for the dead. . . Even the dead (as revenant) does not speak in the name of the dead (as undead); even the ghost, ostensibly a revenant, is not allowed to speak about himself or herself as dead, to fully be his or her own emissary." Ibid., 54.

27. Lancione and Simone, "Tacit Alliances," 12.

---

28. Nichanian, "Catastrophic Mourning," 109.

29. AbdouMaliq Simone, *Improvised Lives: Rhythms of Endurance in an Urban South* (Cambridge, UK: Polity, 2018), 68–69.

30. Simone, *Improvised Lives*, 69.

31. Ibid., 126.

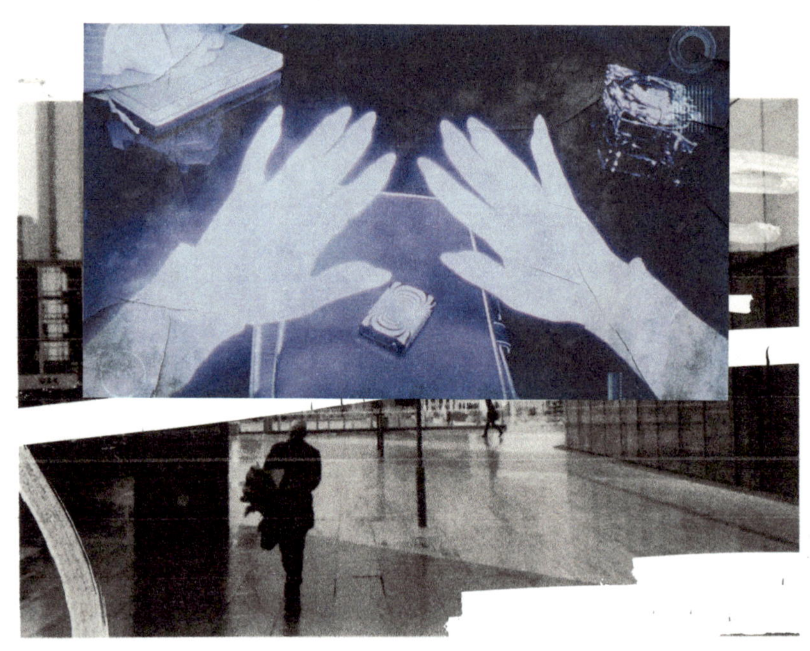

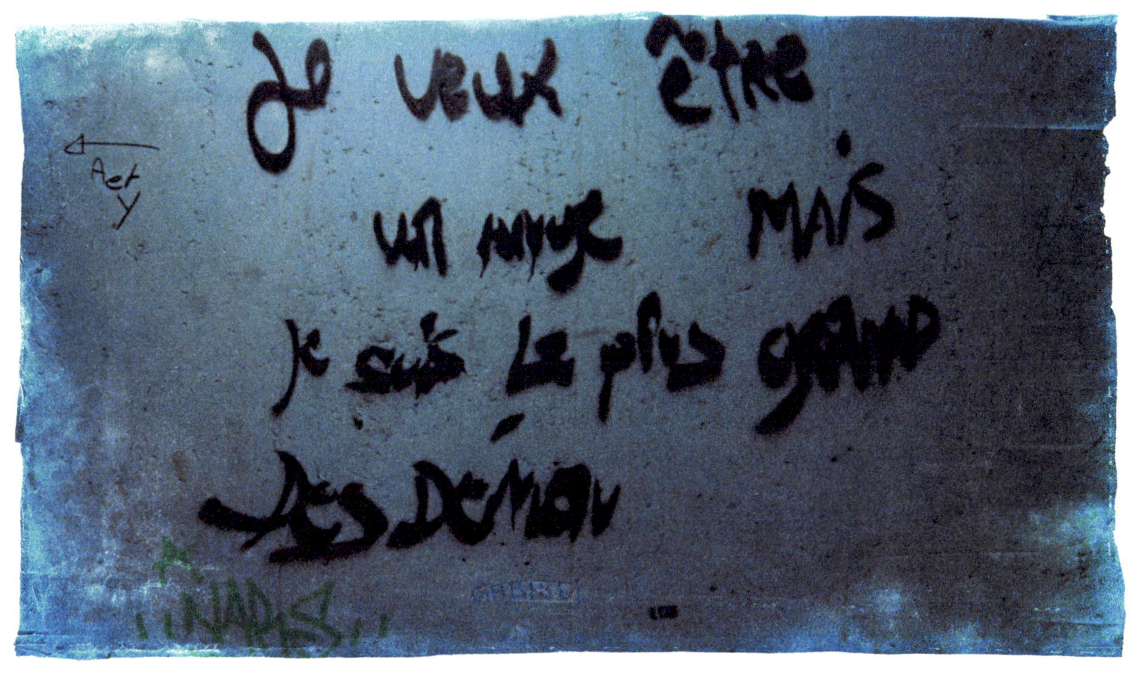

Je veux être
un nuage   mais
je suis le plus grand
des démon

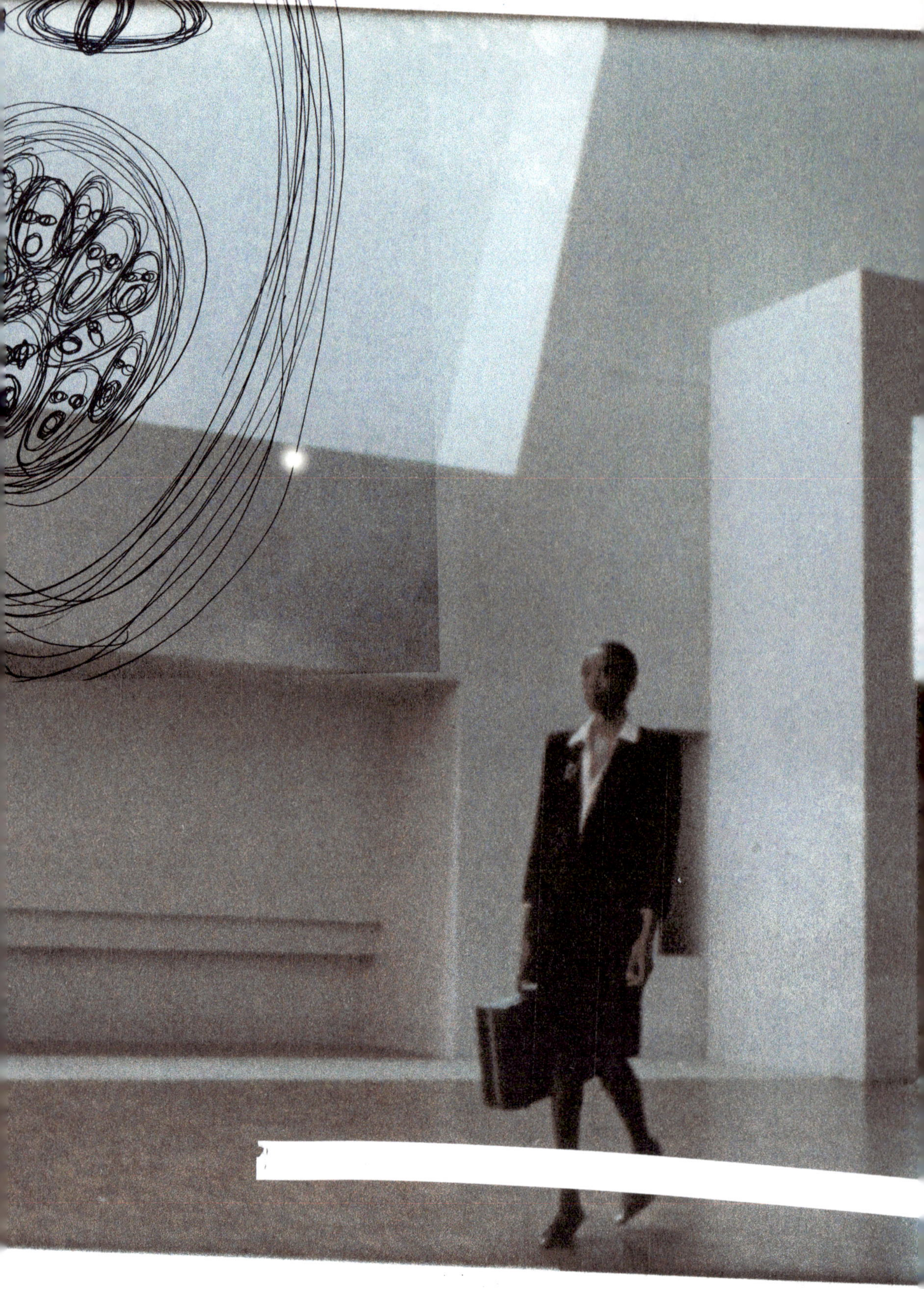

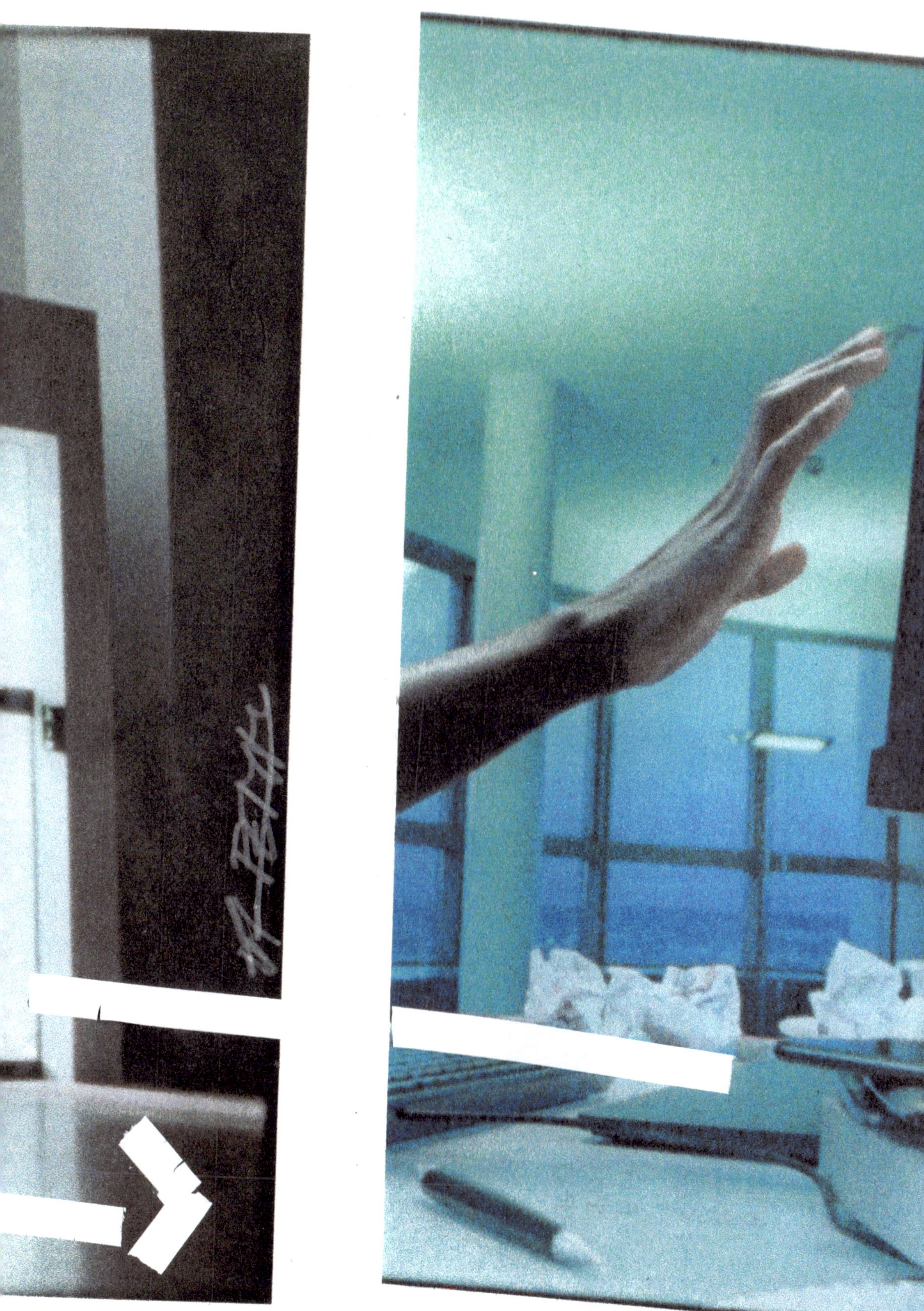

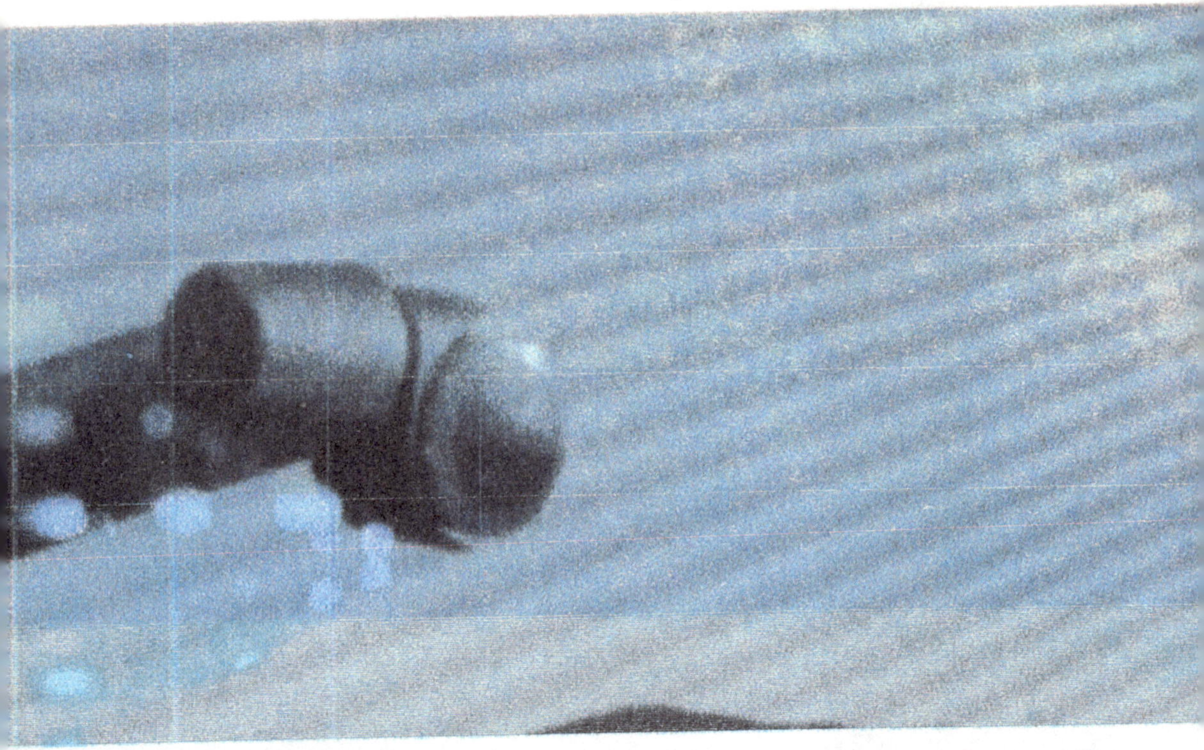

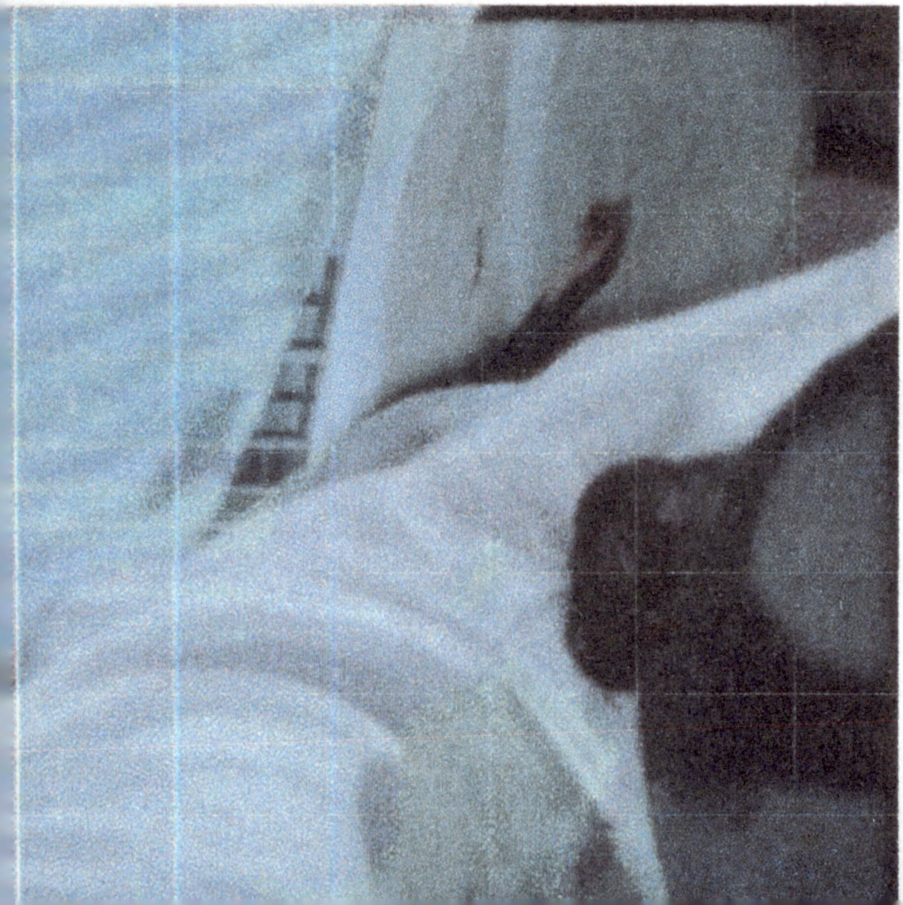

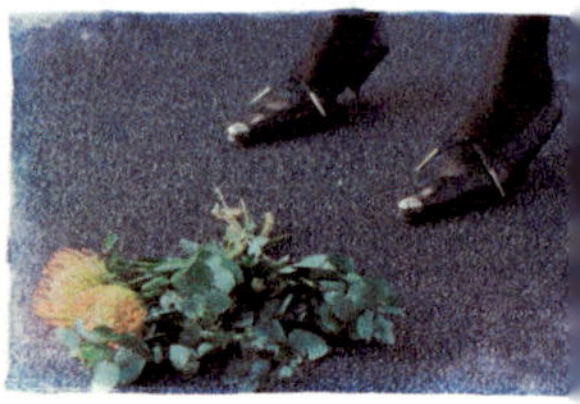

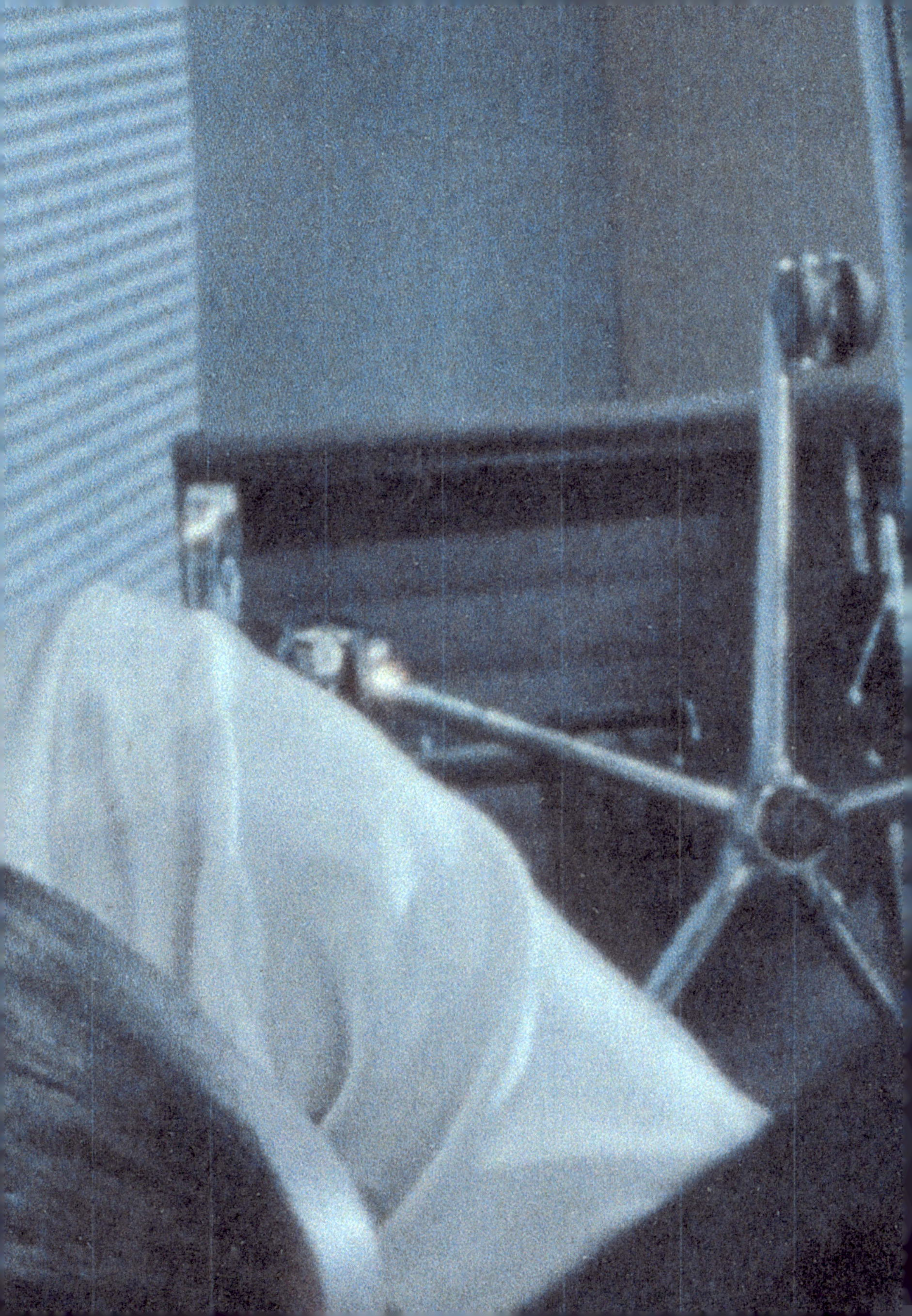

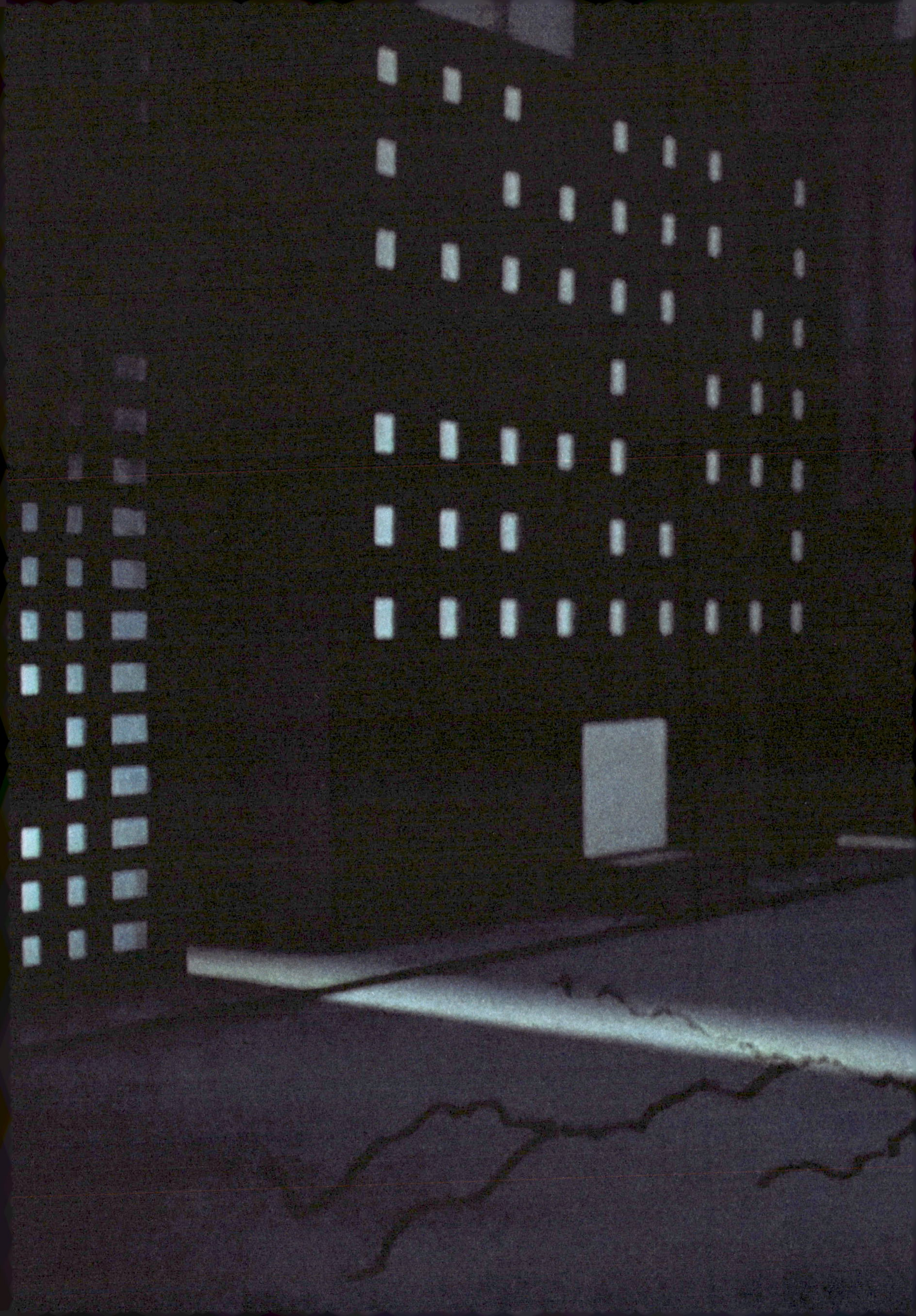

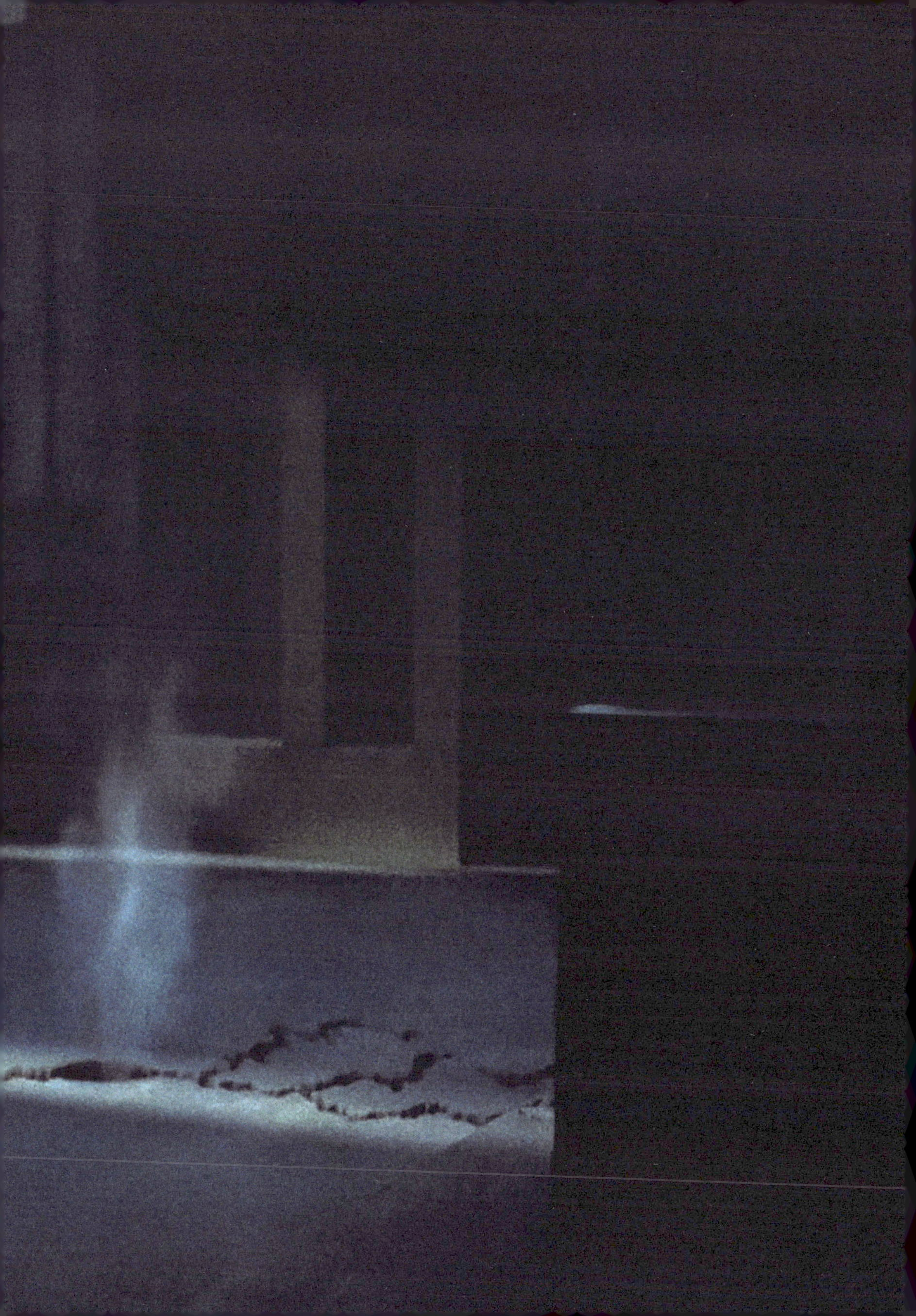

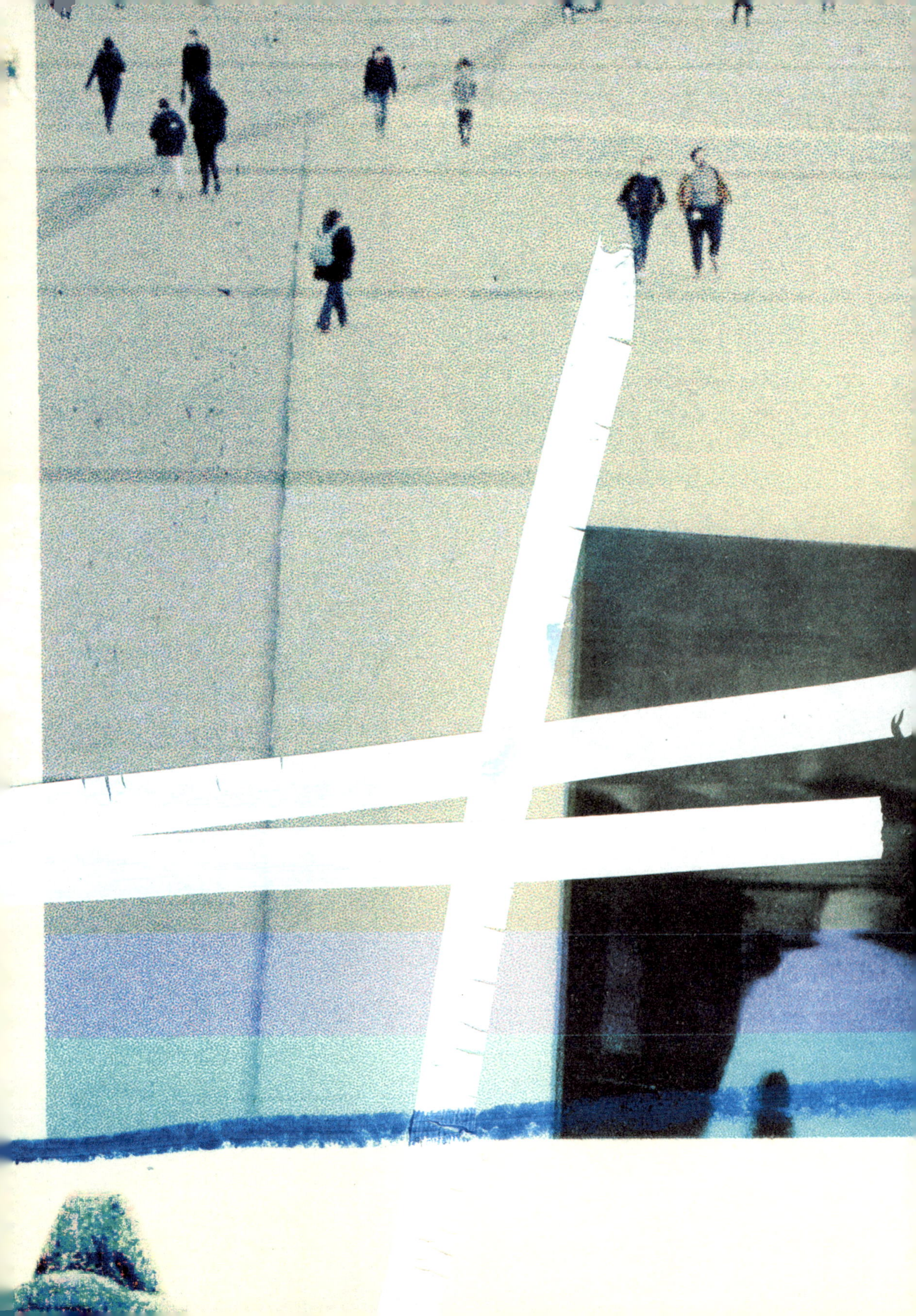

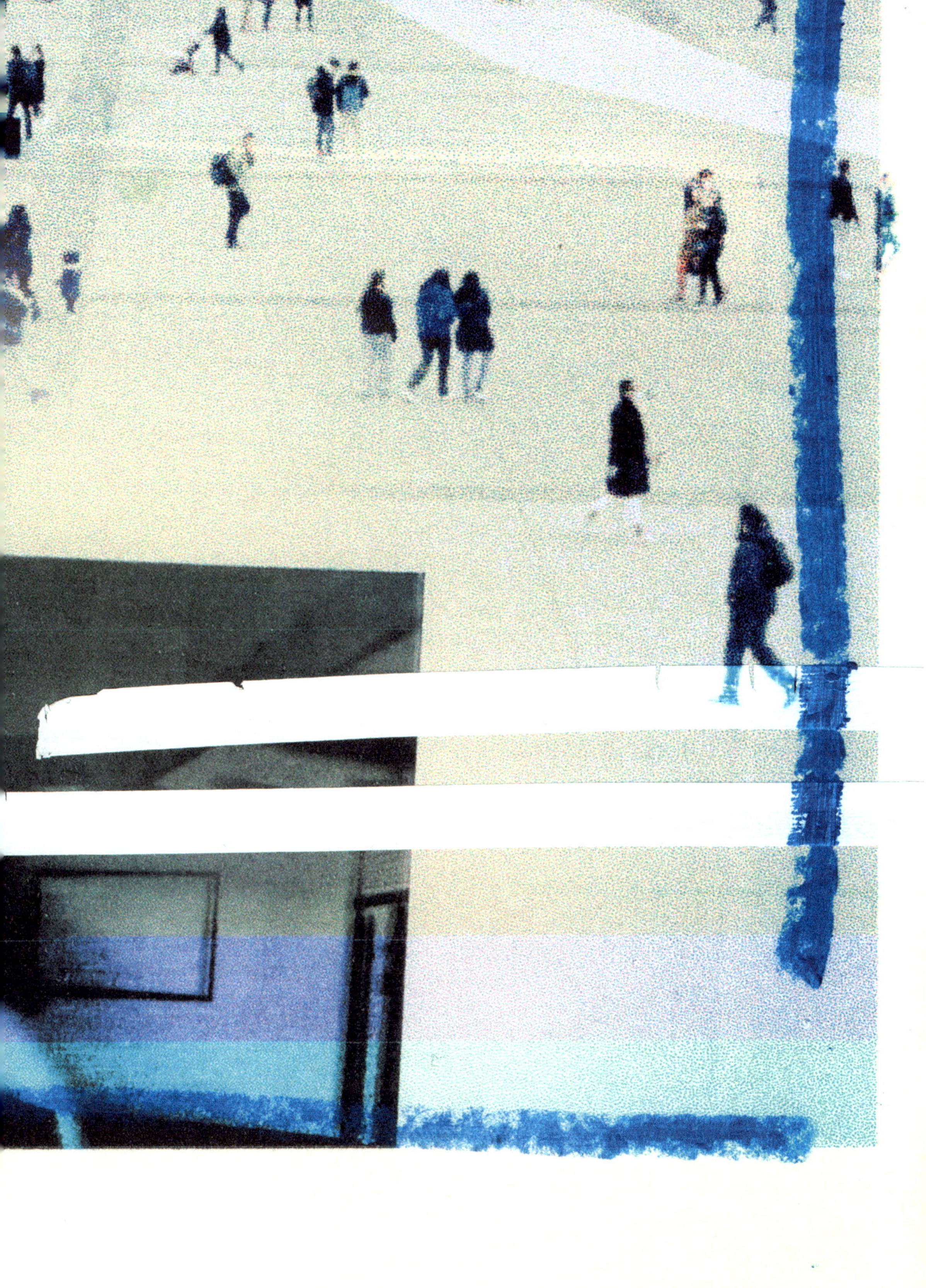

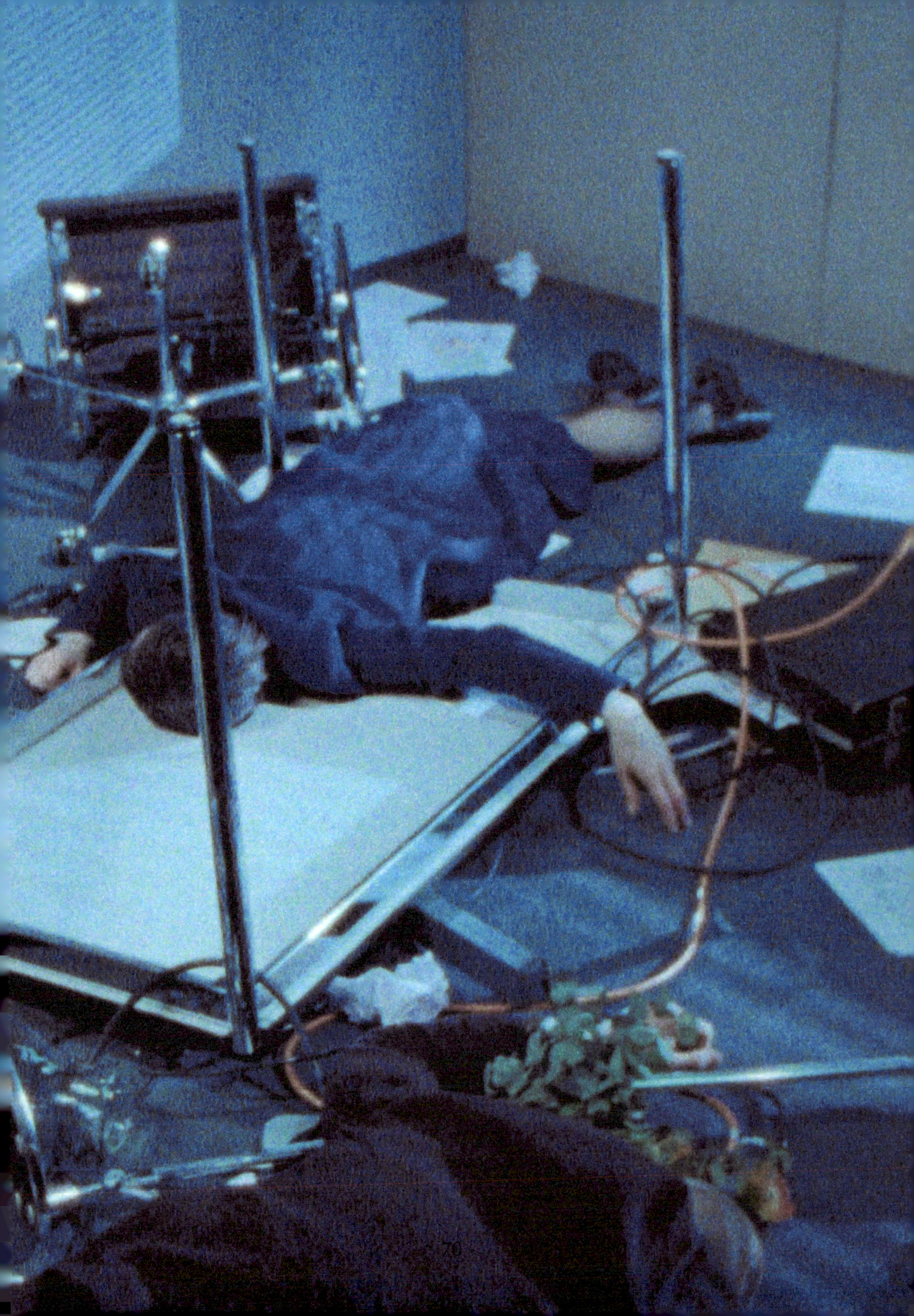

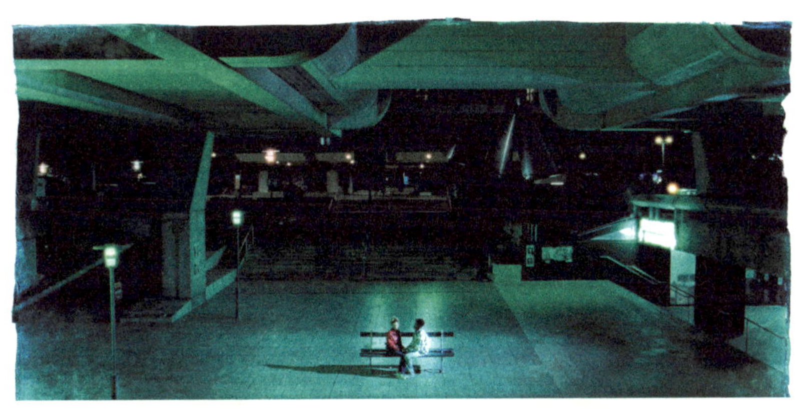

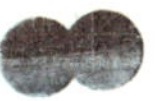

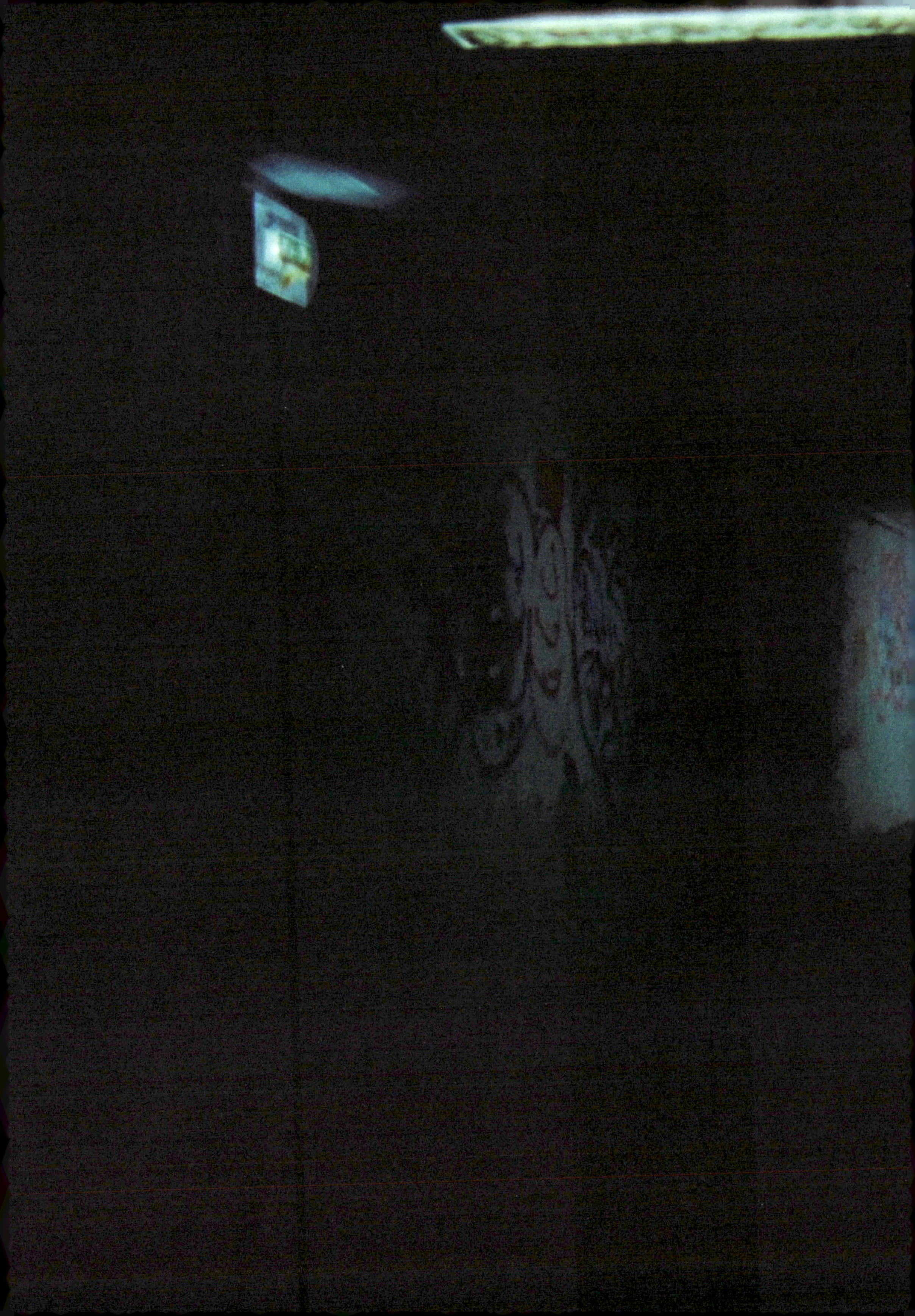

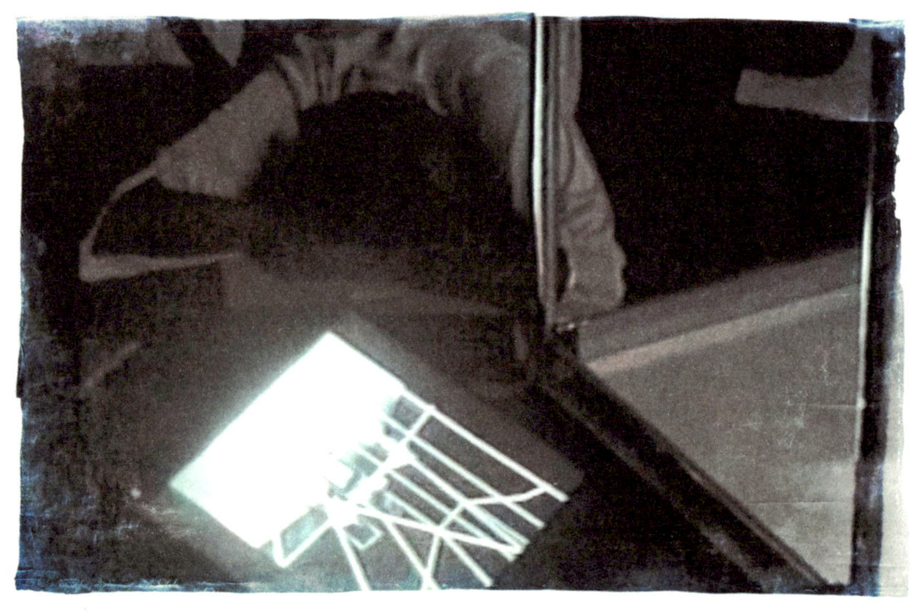

zone
INTERZONE
INTERZONE
INTERZONE
interzon
INTERZONE
INTERZONE

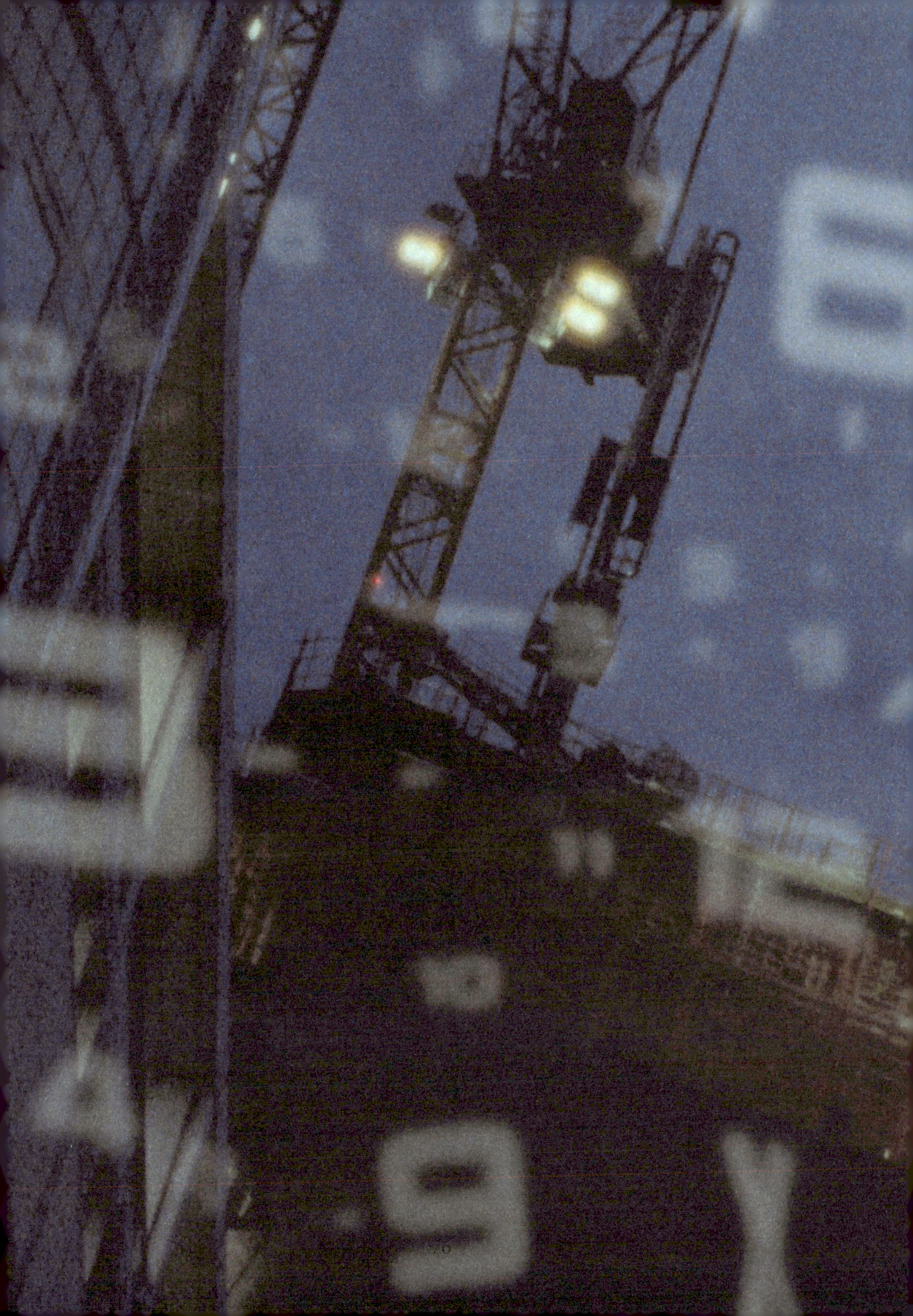

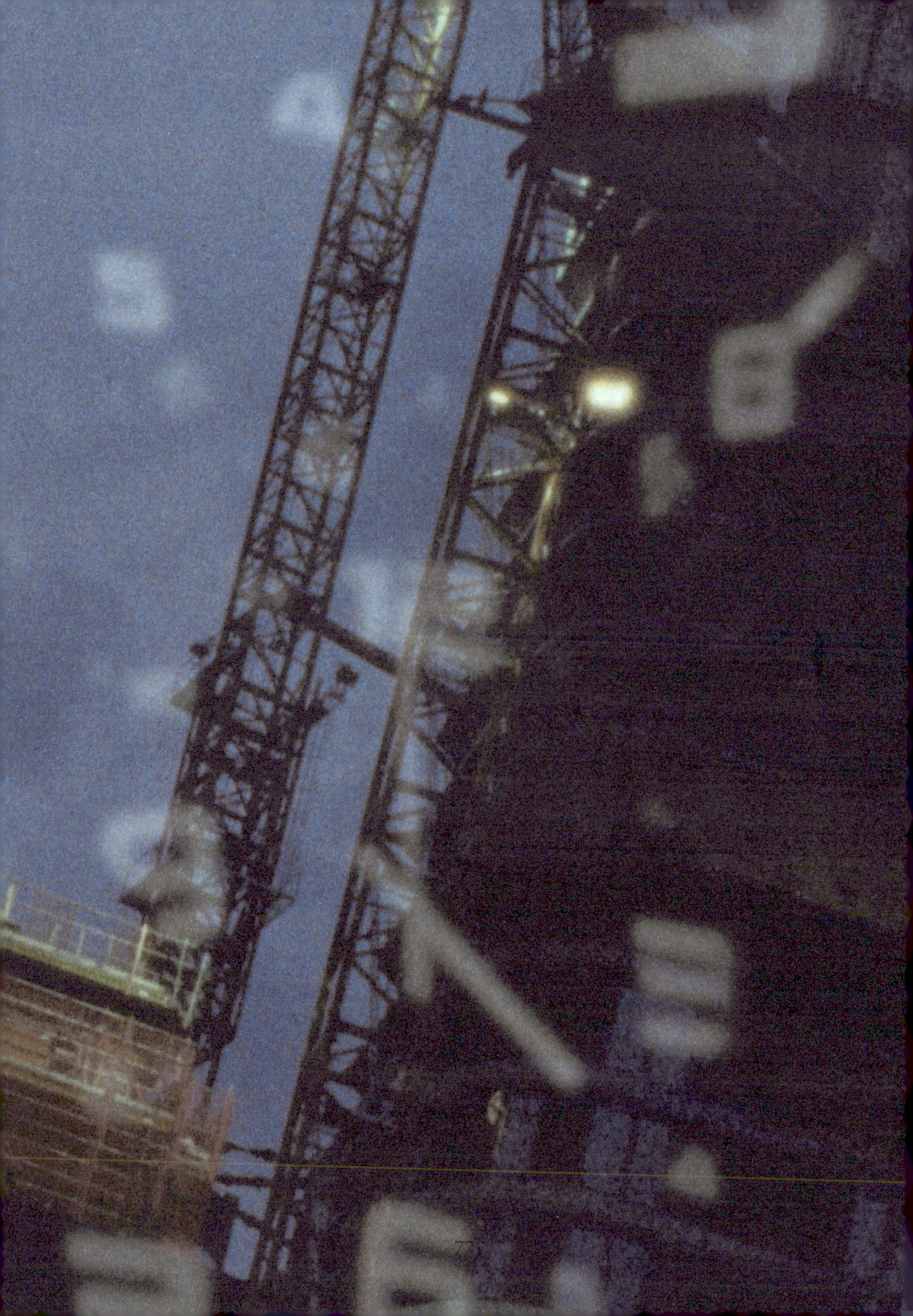

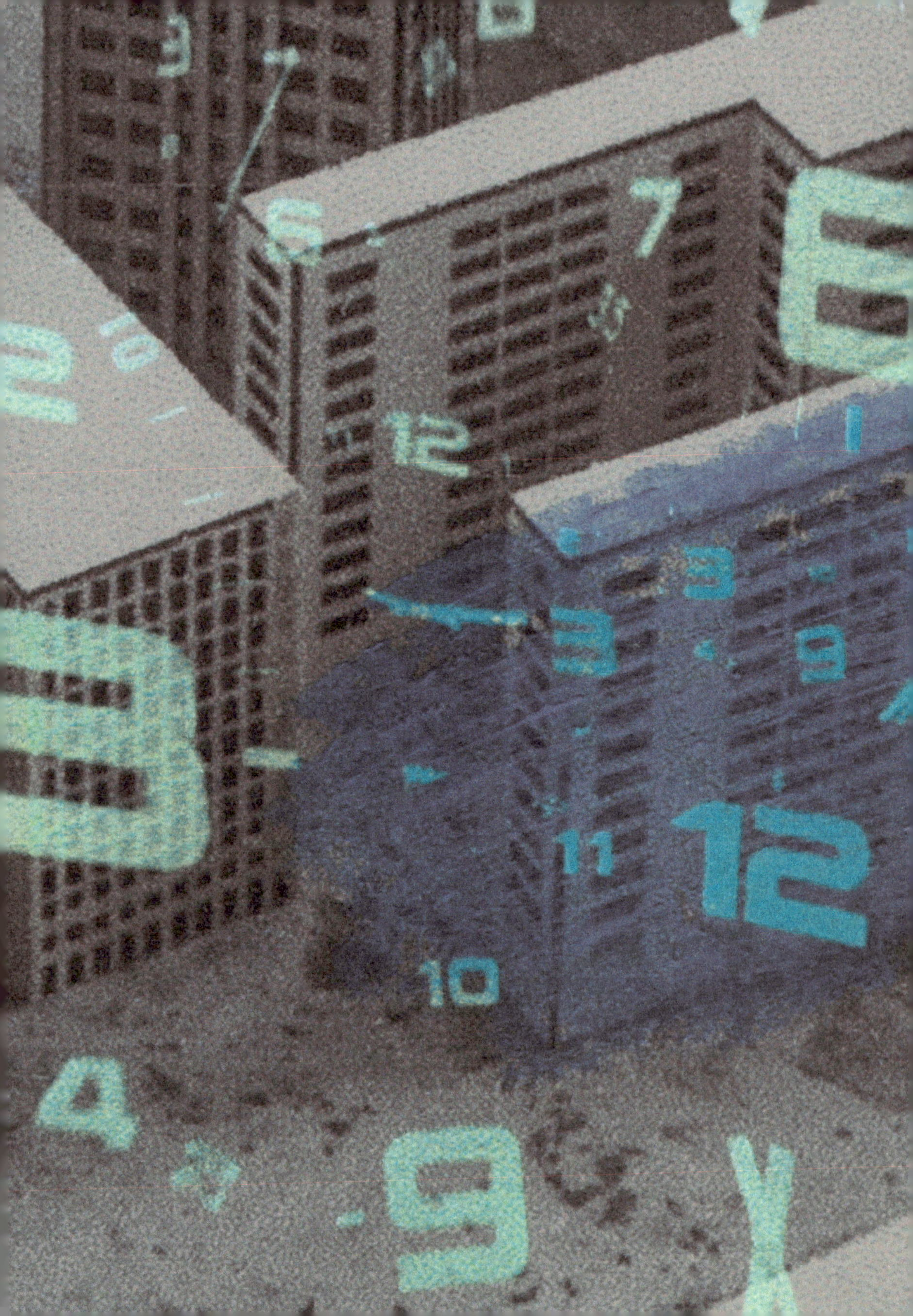

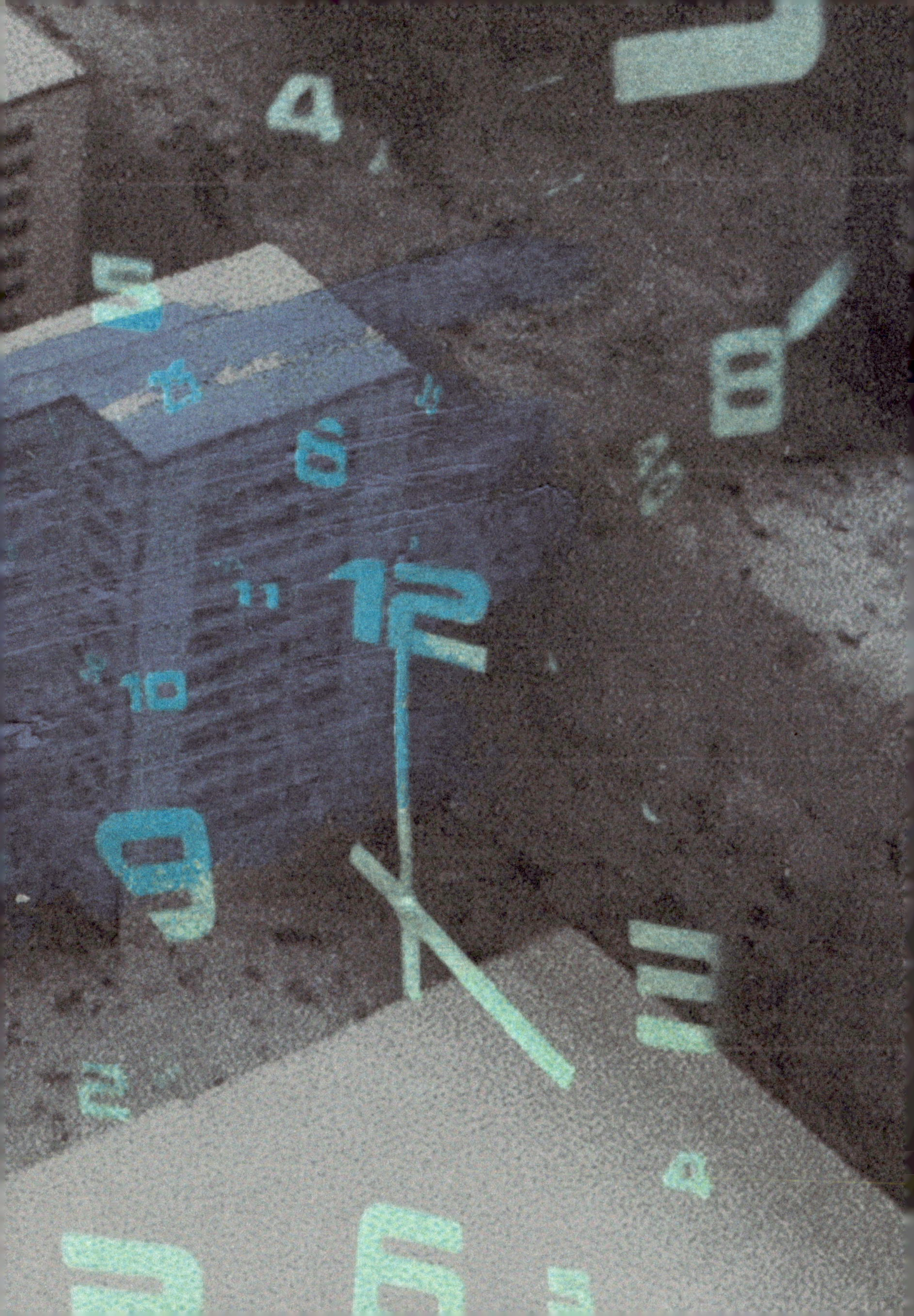

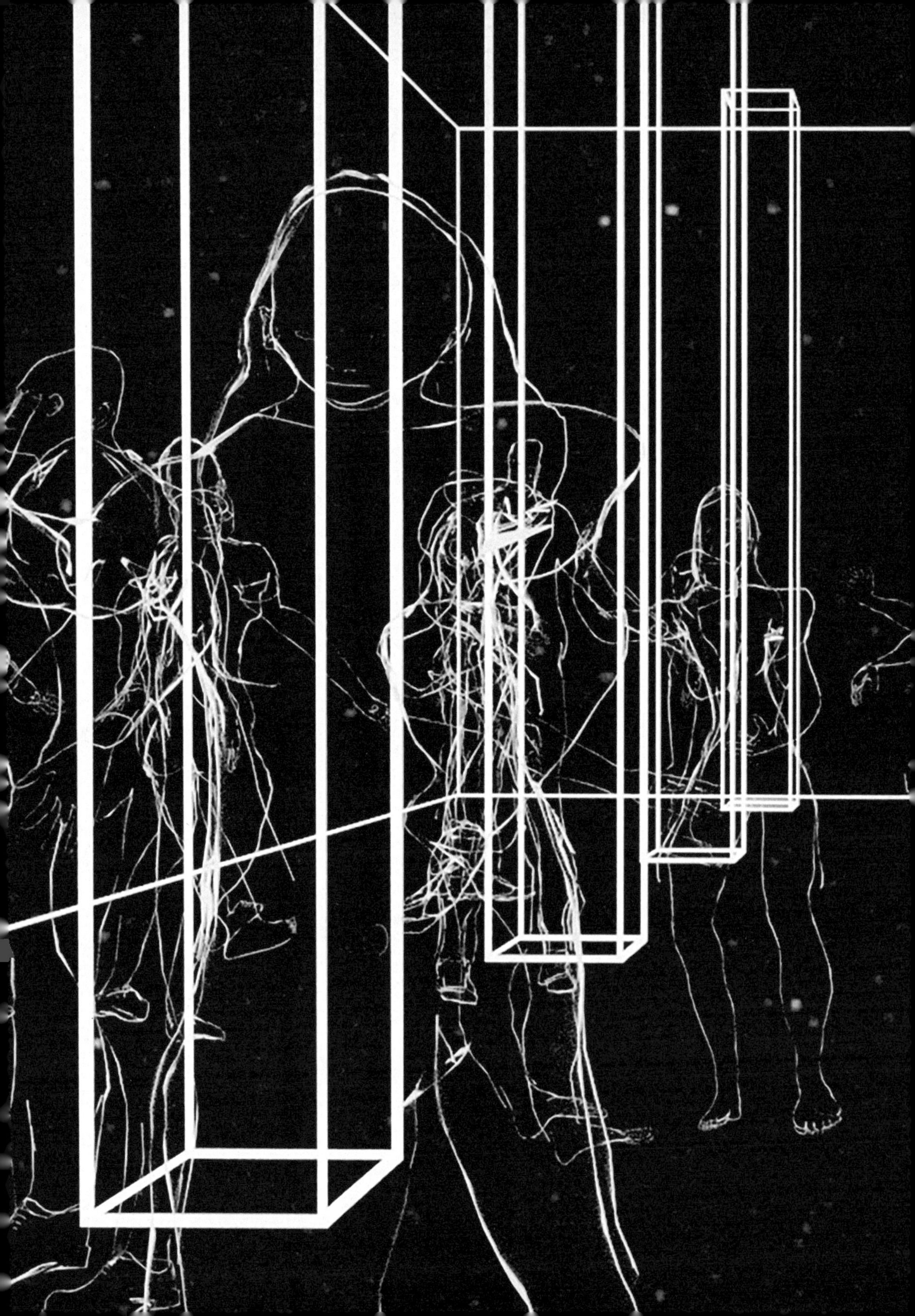

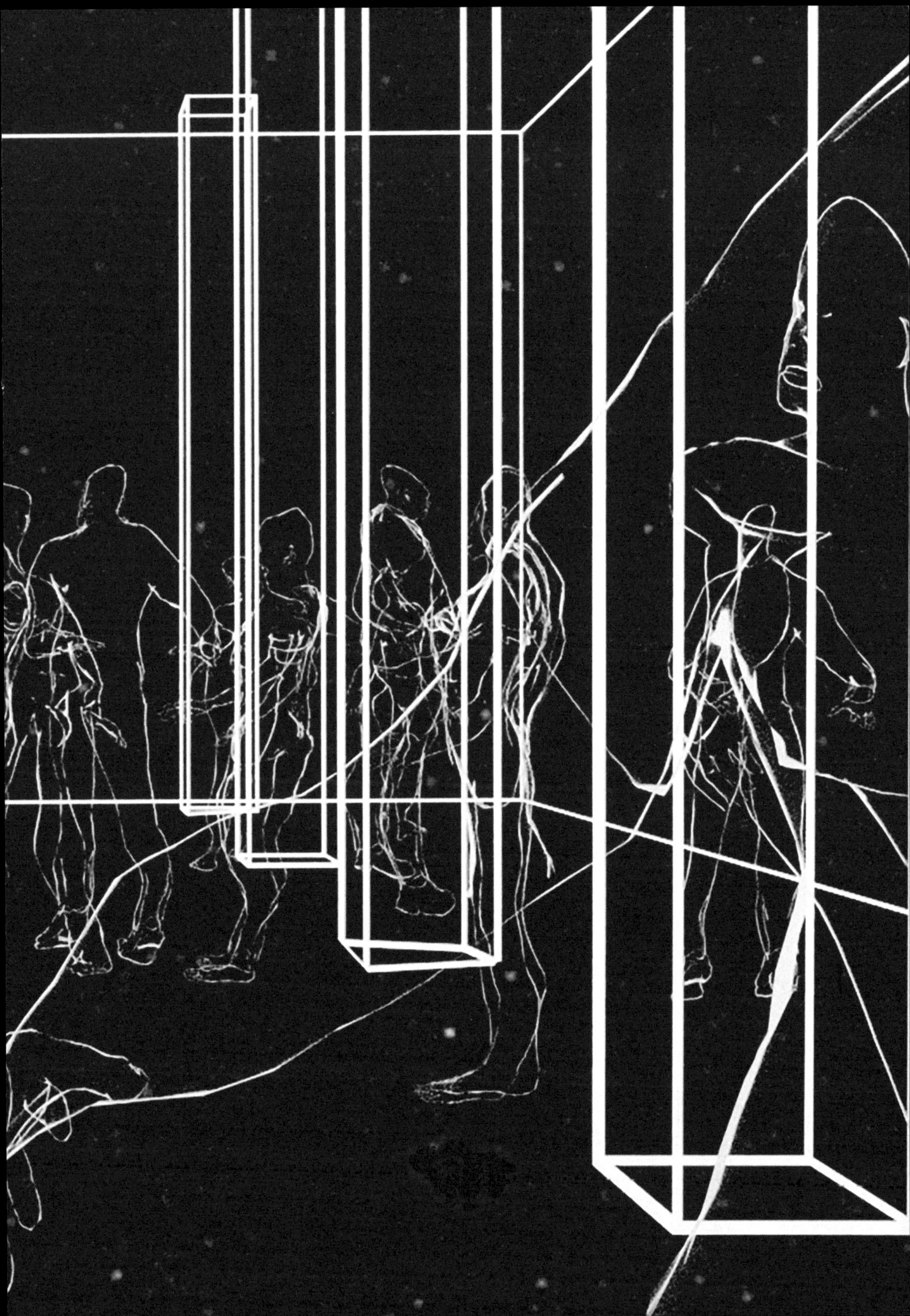

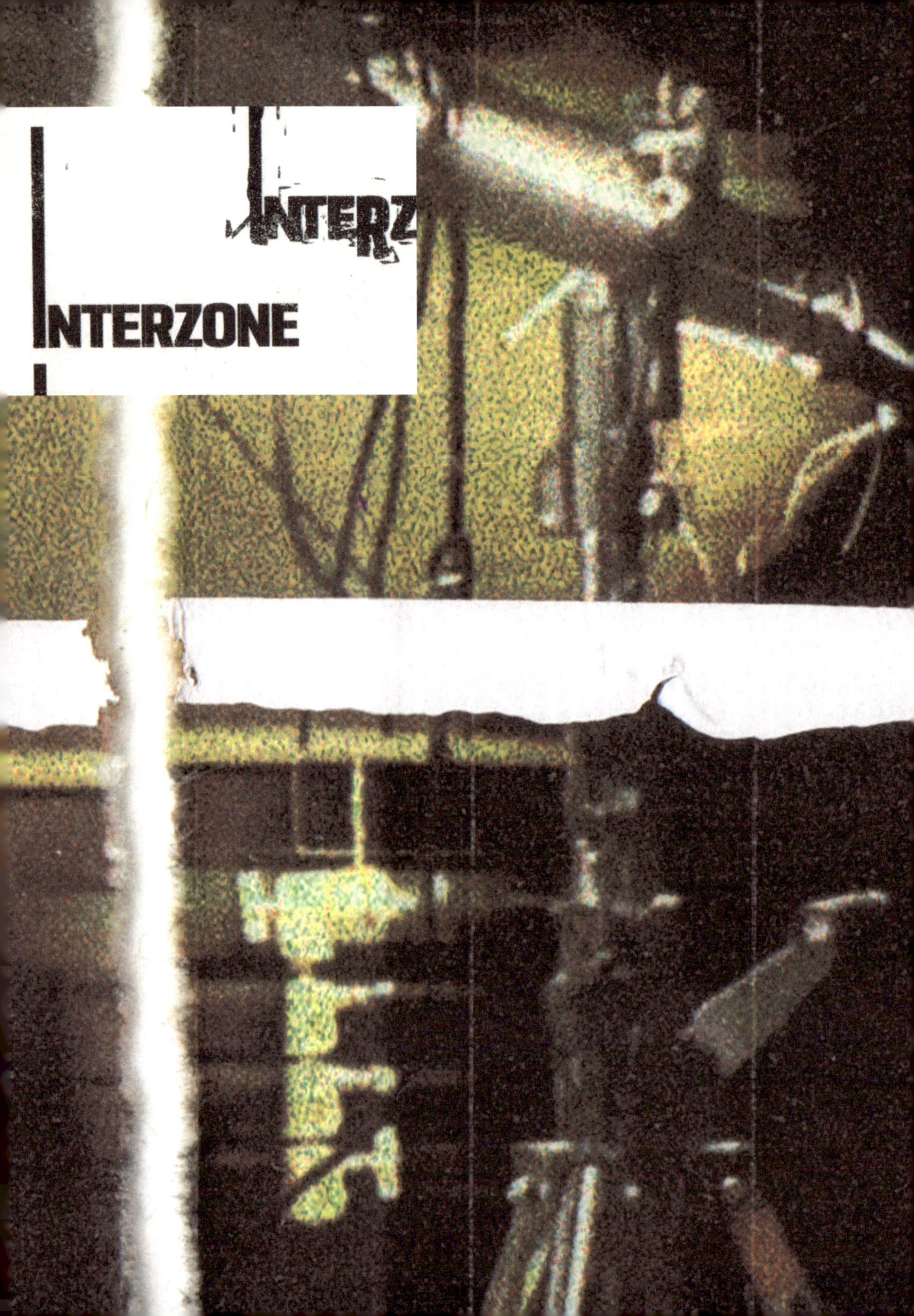
INTERZONE
INTERZONE

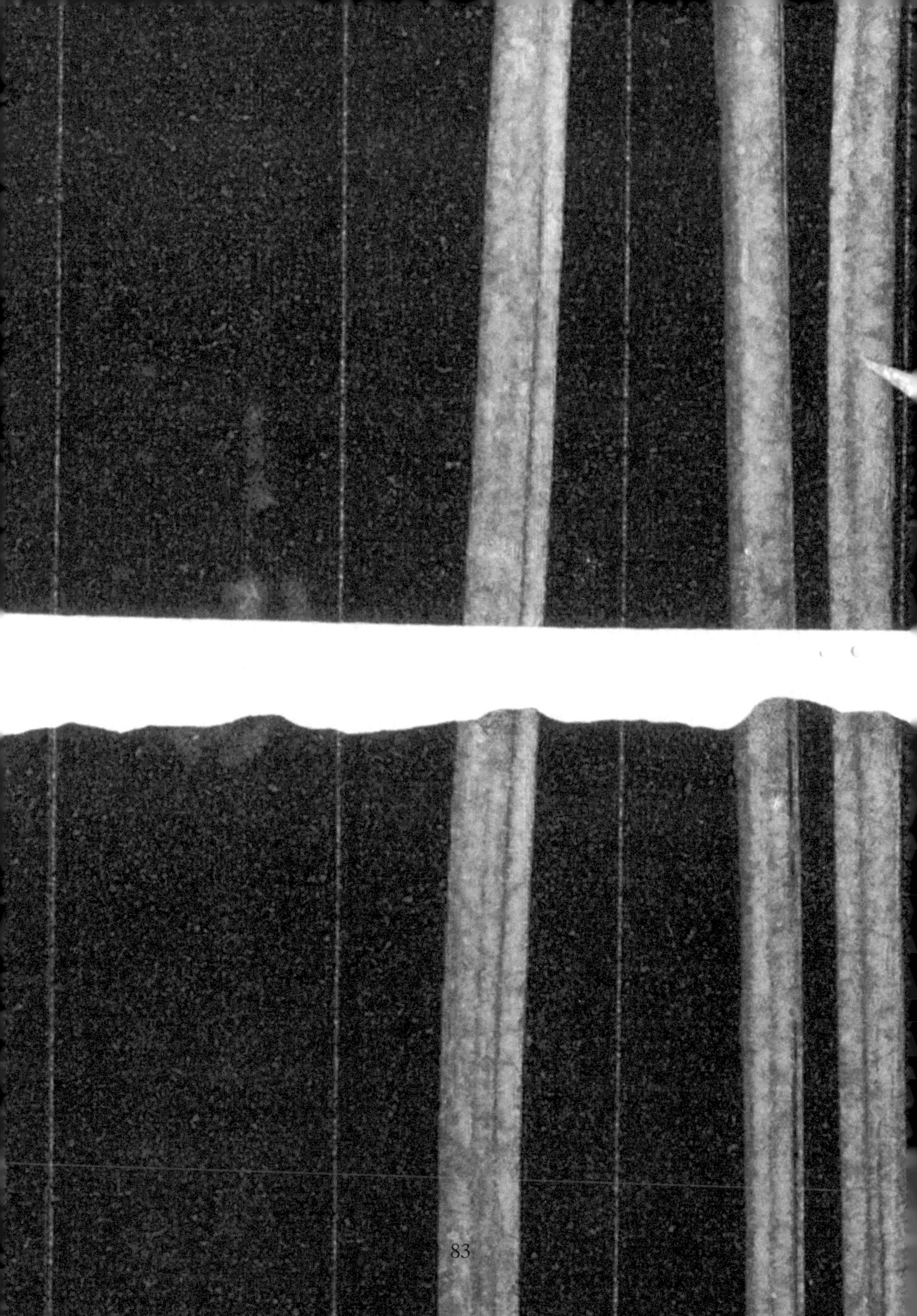

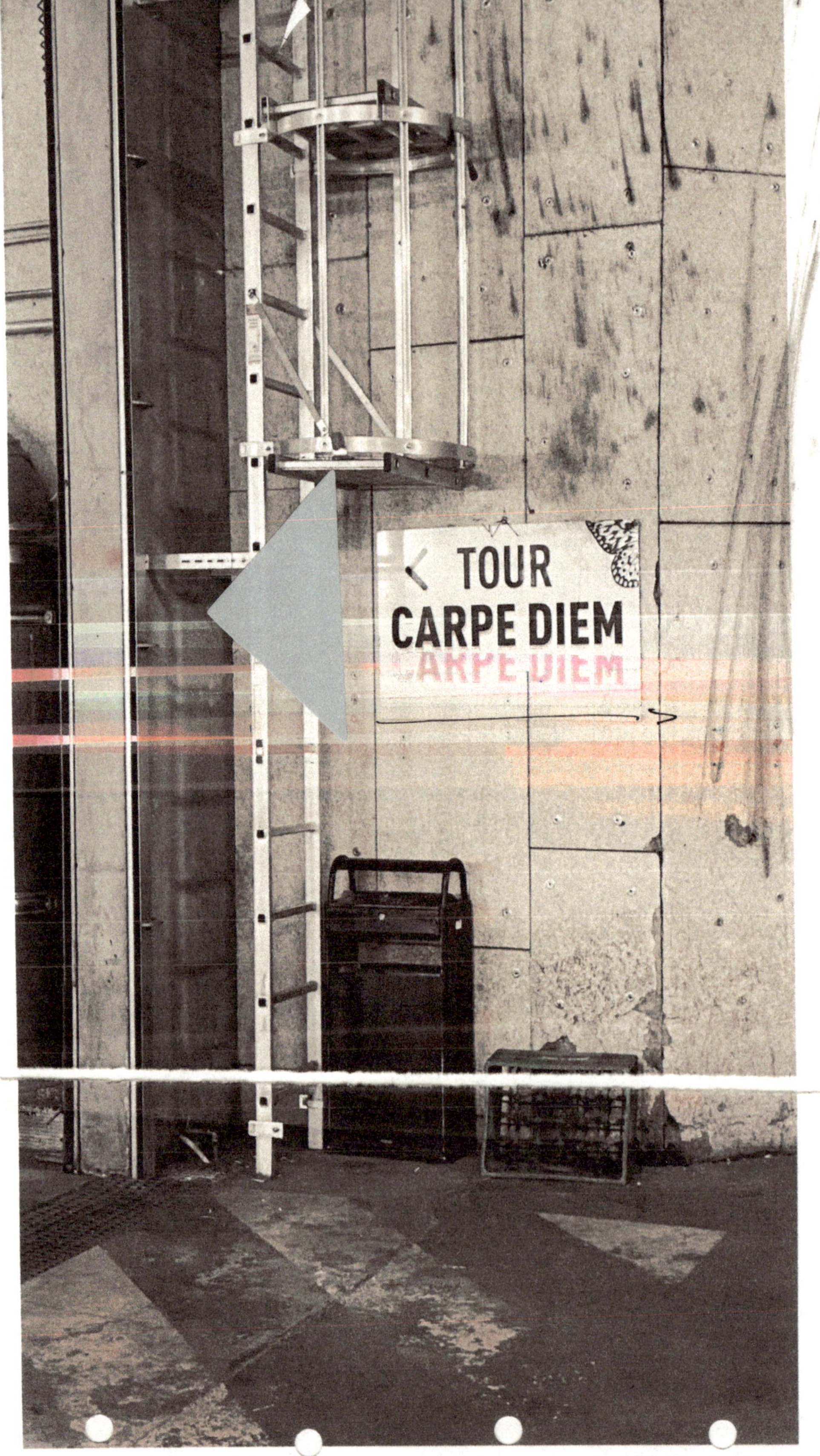

TOUR
CARPE DIEM

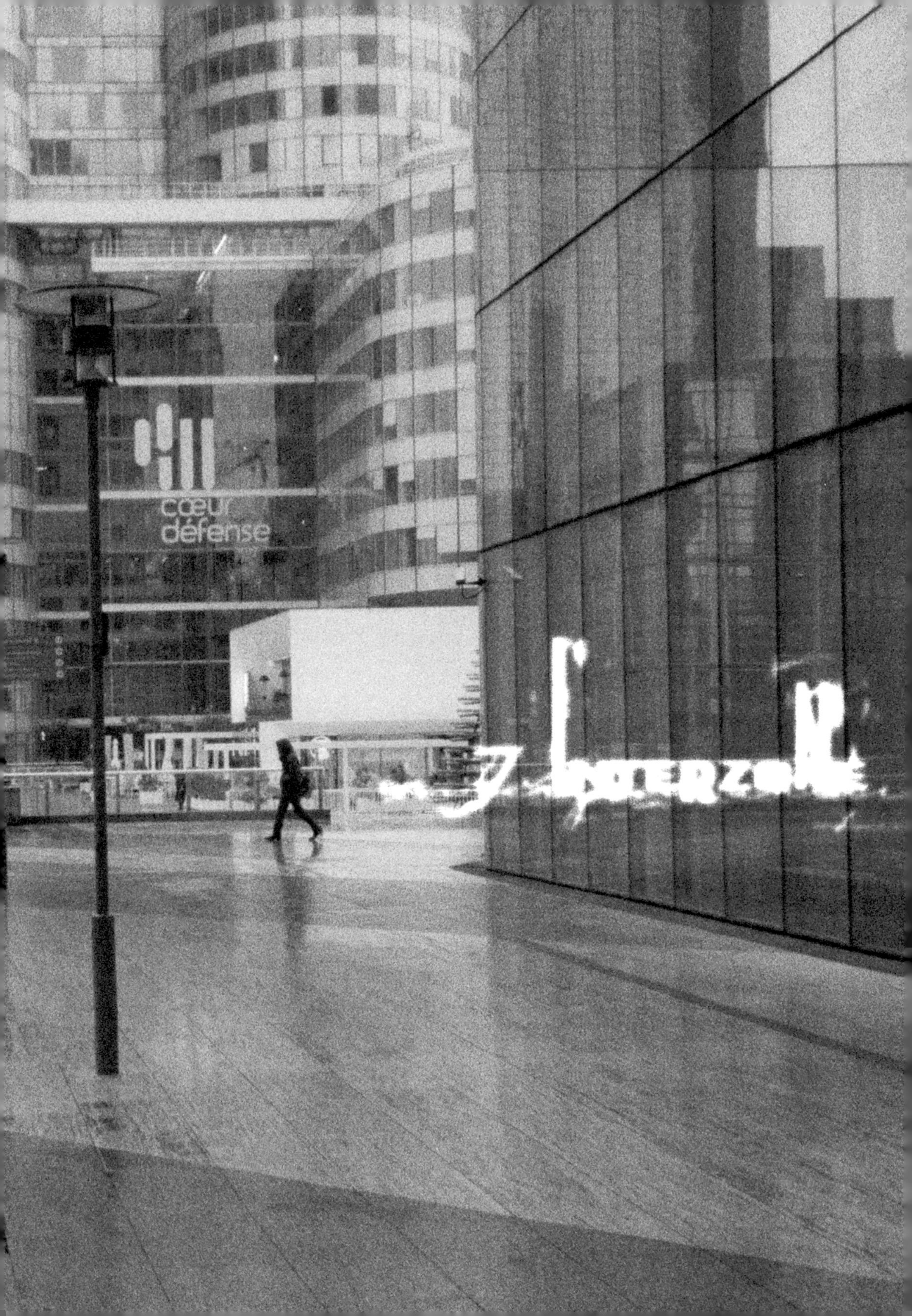

cœur
défense

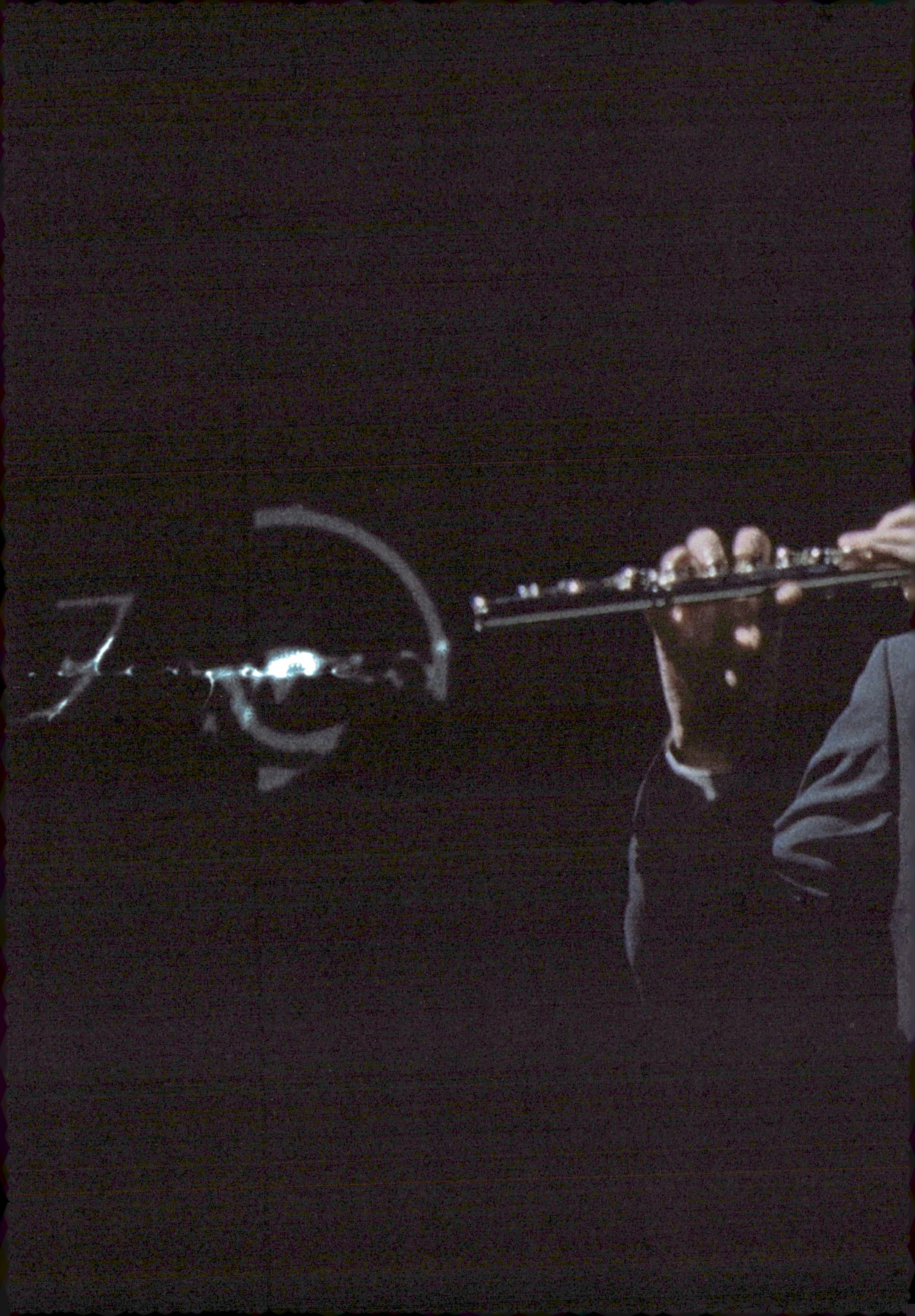

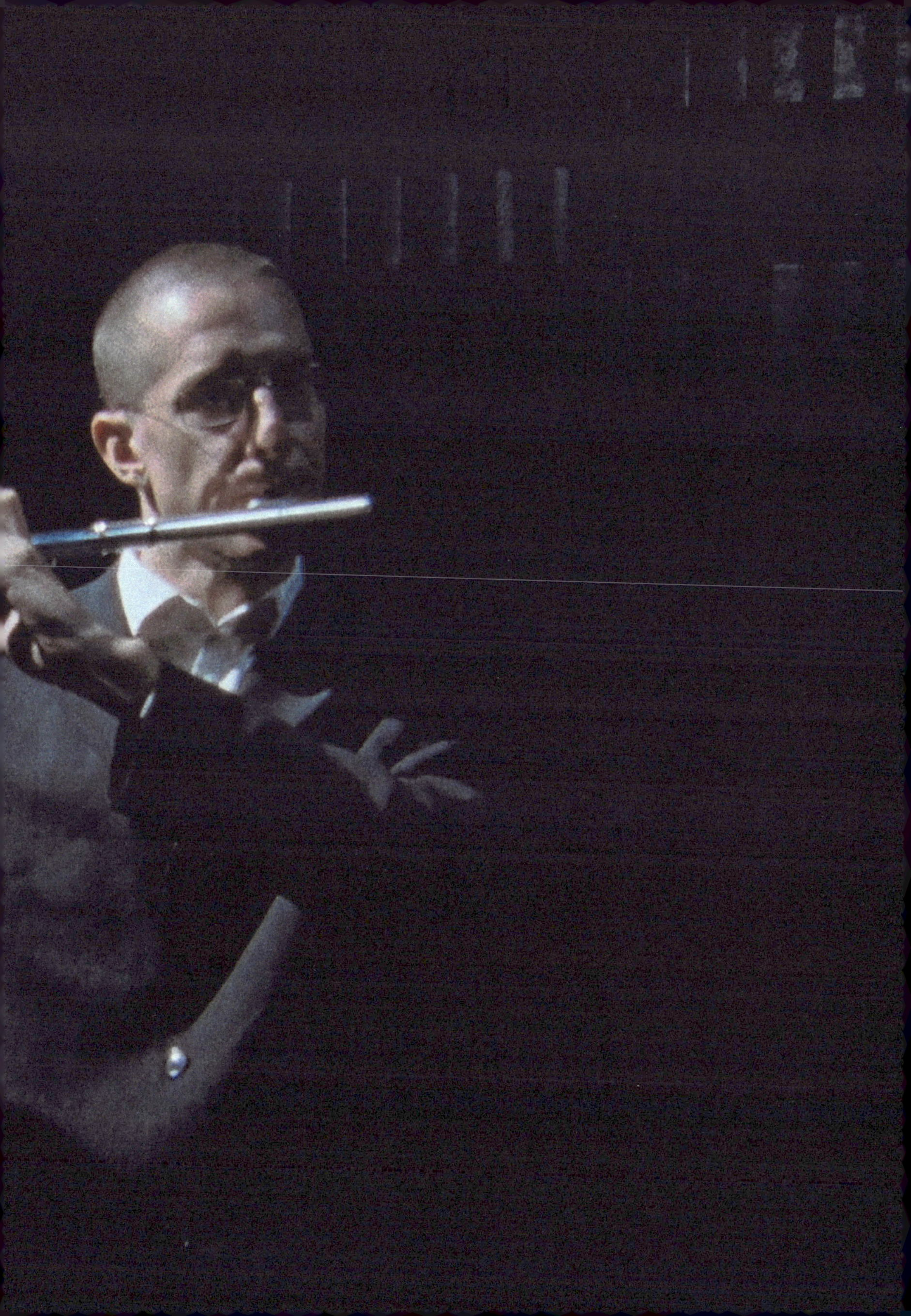

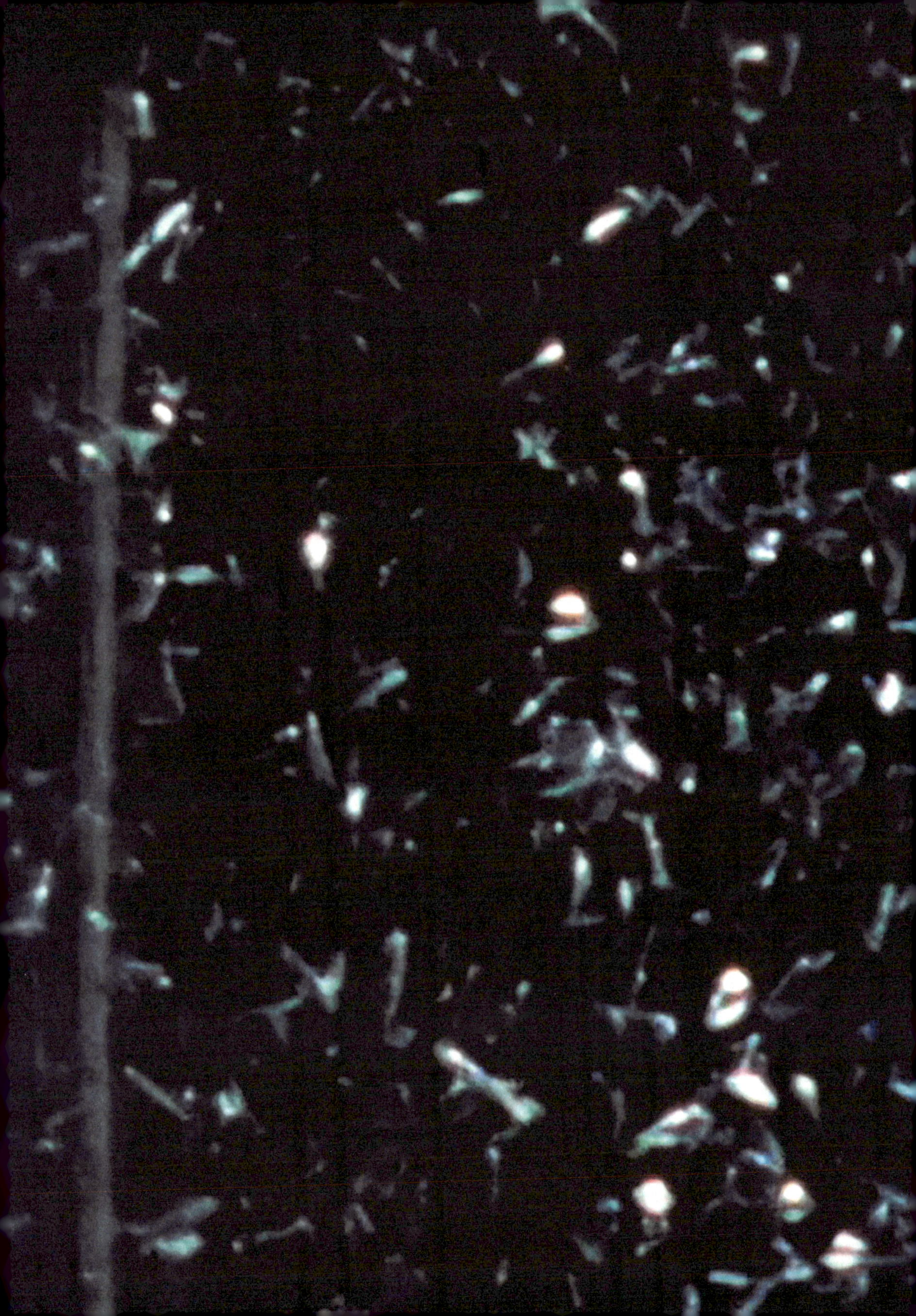

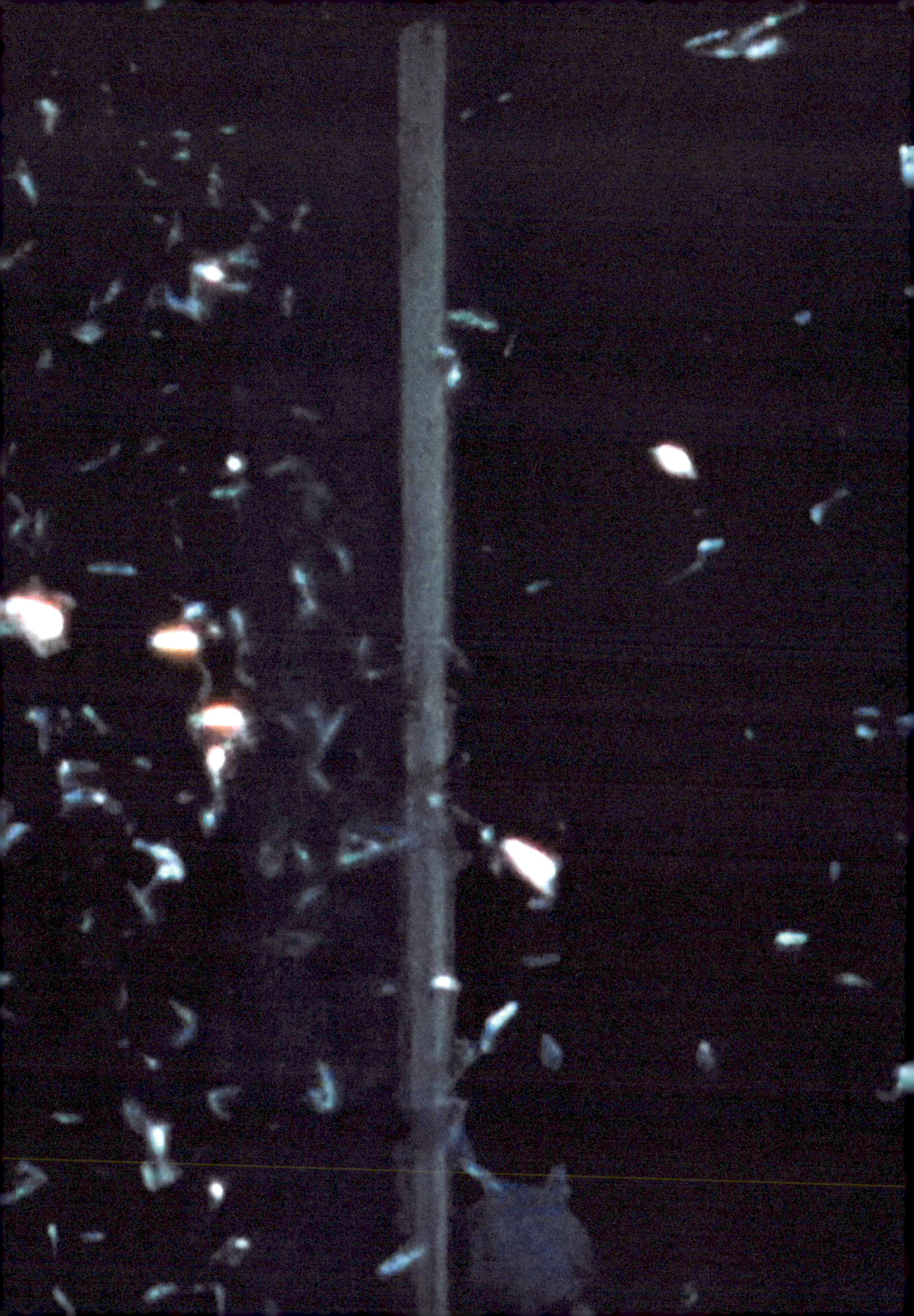

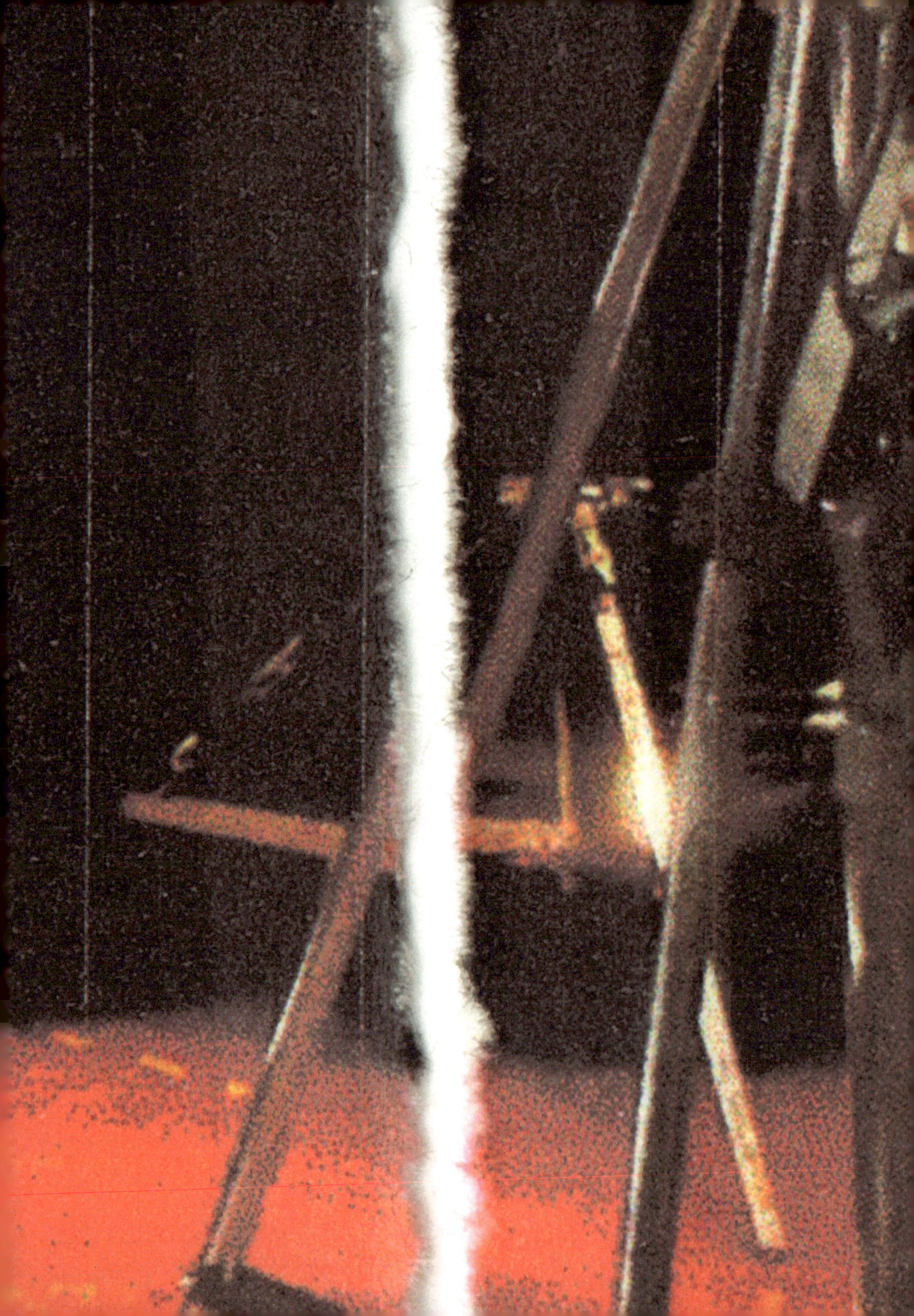

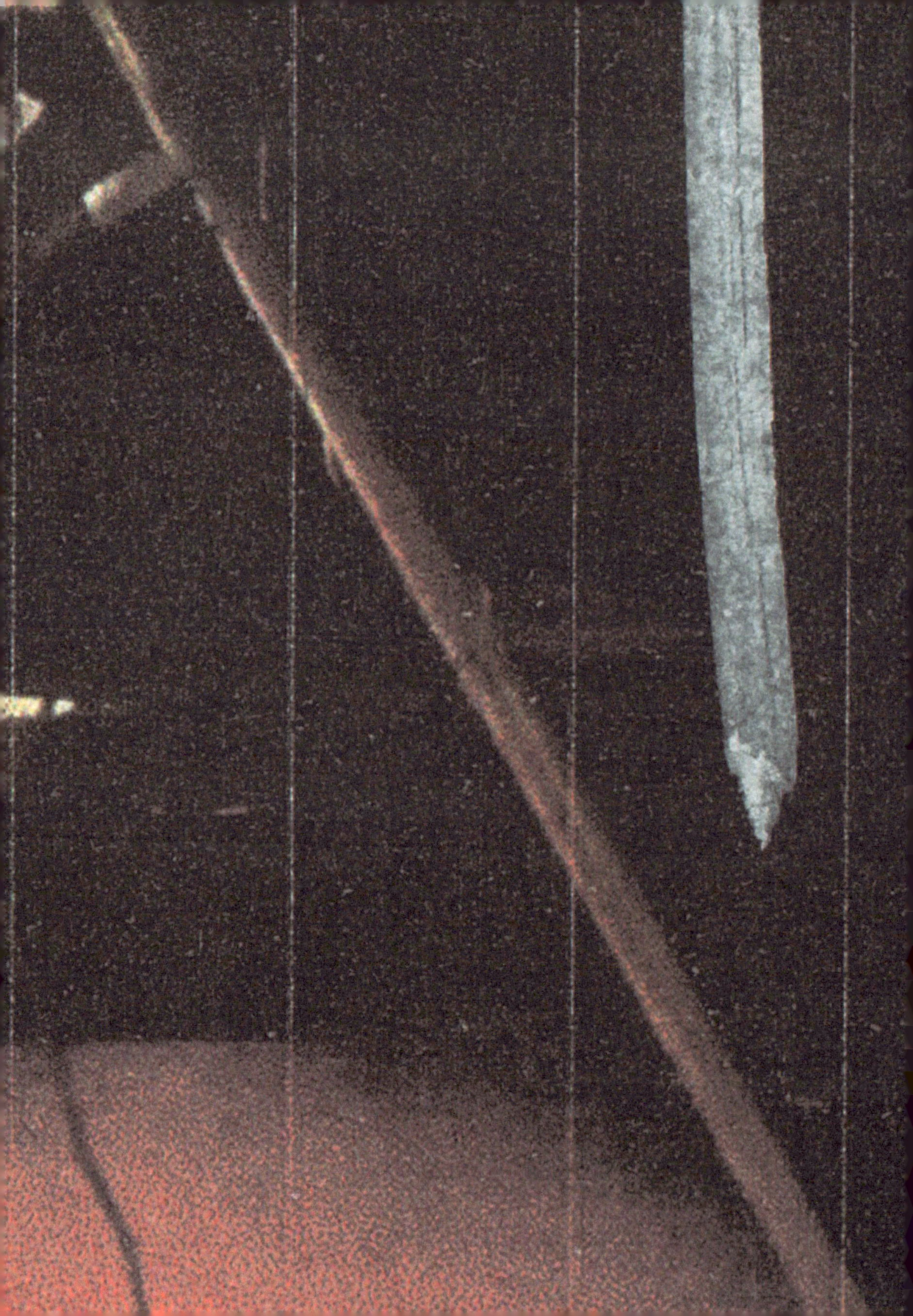

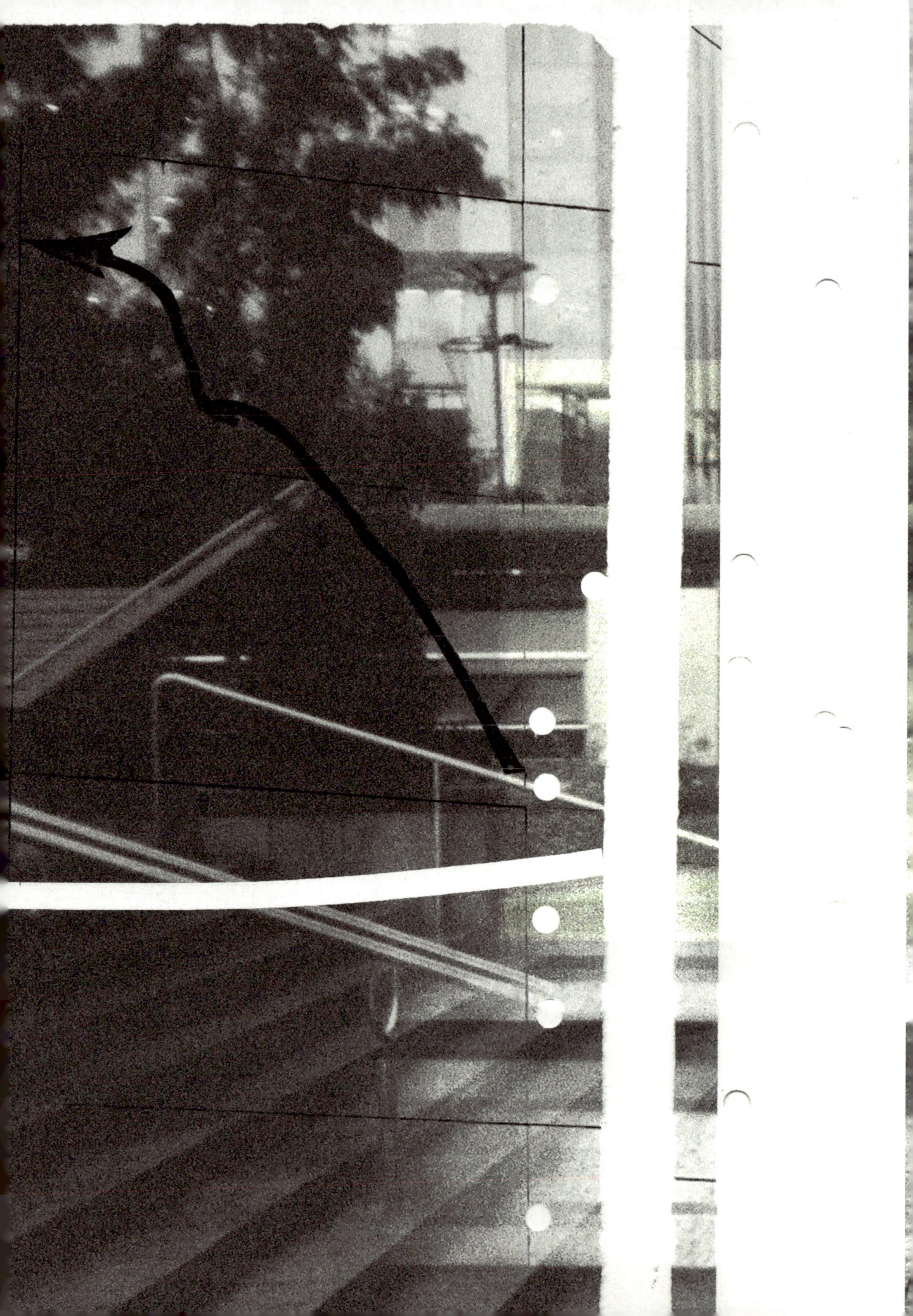

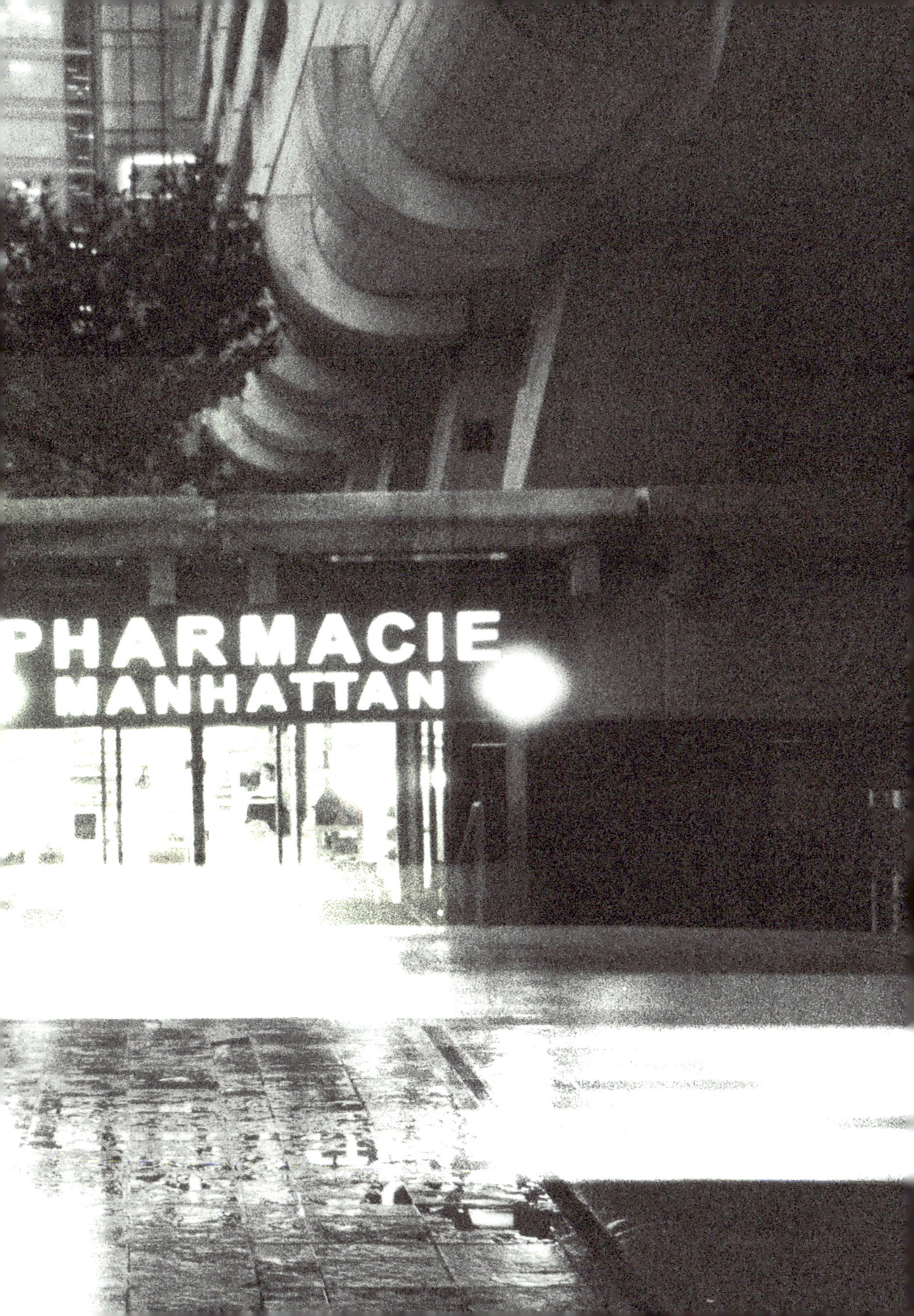

PHARMACIE
MANHATTAN

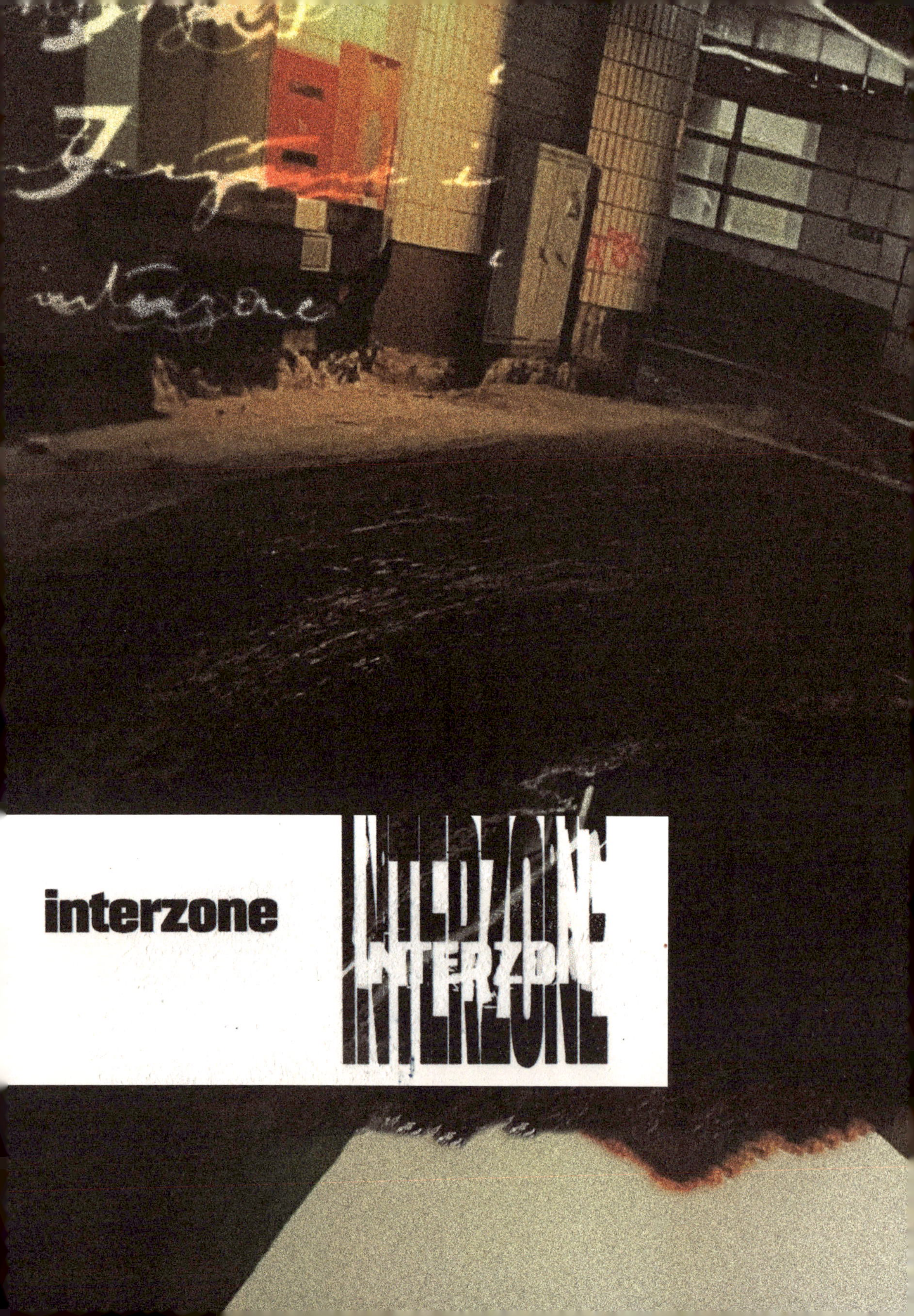
interzone
INTERZONE
INTERZONE

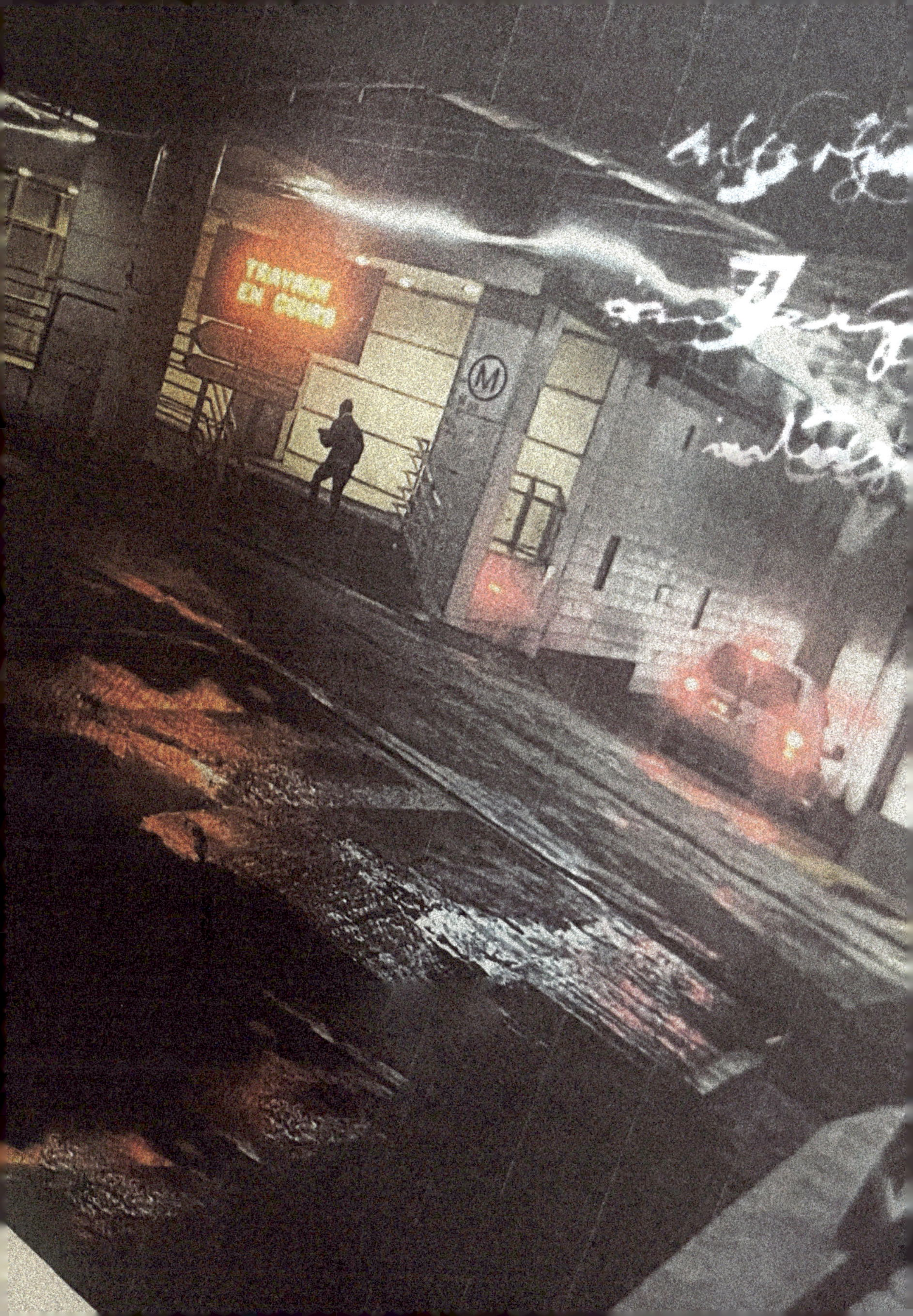
TRAVAUX
EN COURS
M

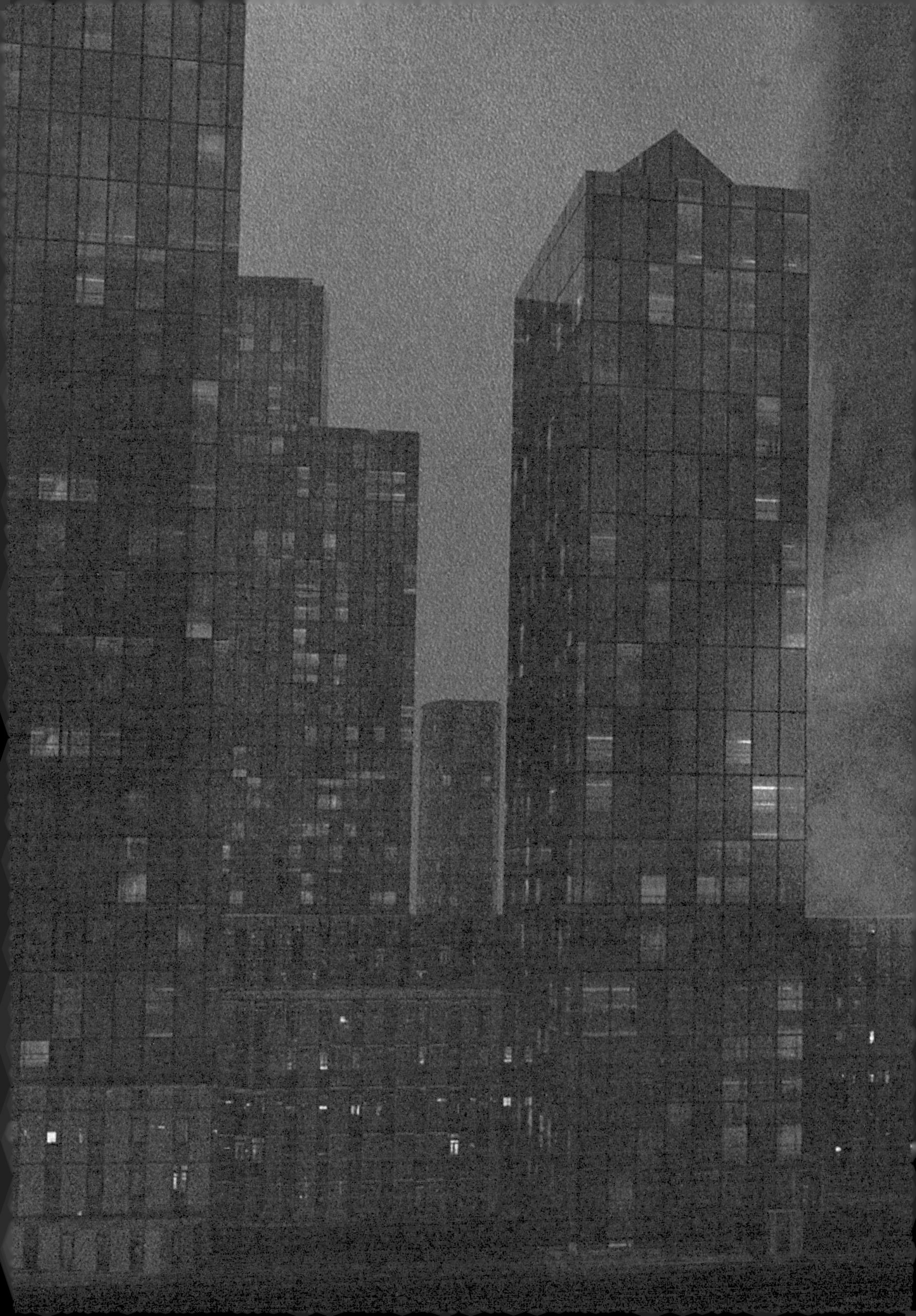

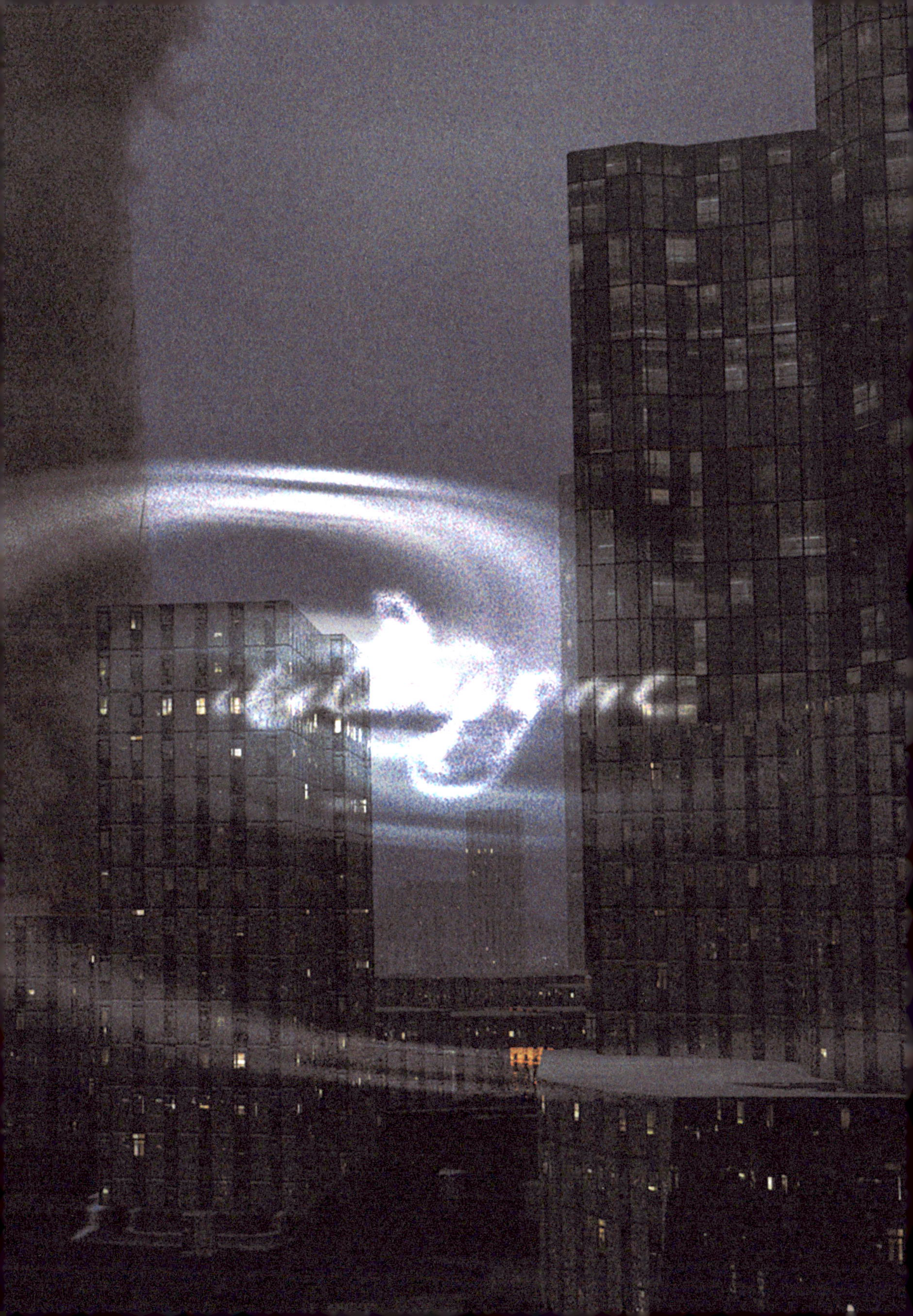

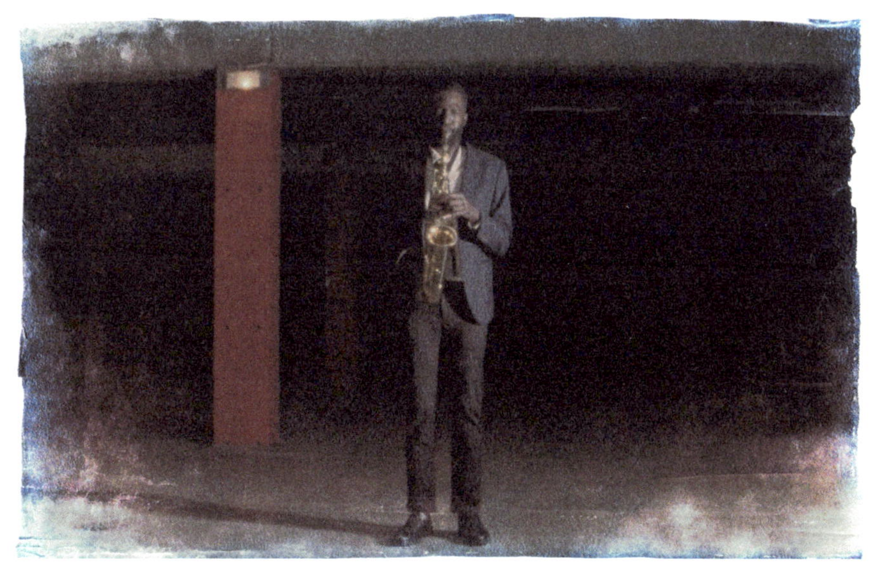

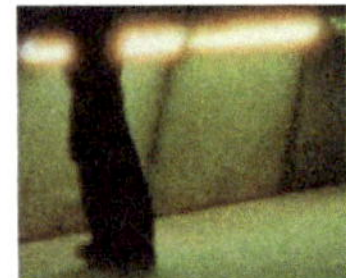

INT. NIGHT. A door opens in an empty parking lot. Someone is waiting.

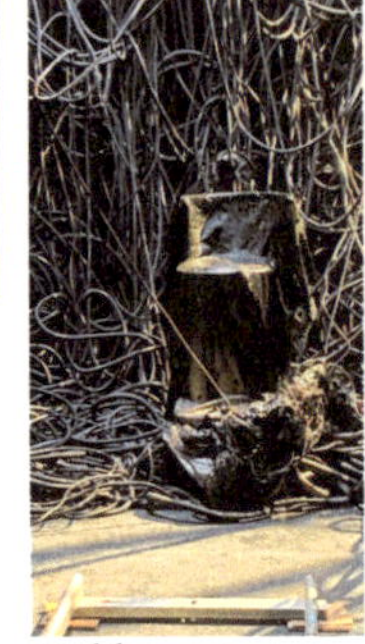

Cable nest. The belly of the architect. Something is growing in there.

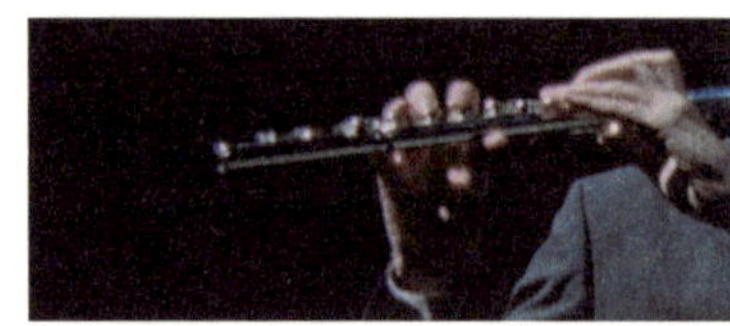

Left hand. Shallow breath–might be broken?

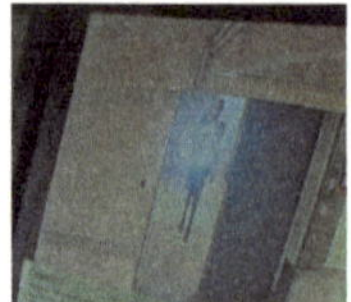

INT. OFFICE. NIGHT OR DAY? Nothing moves.

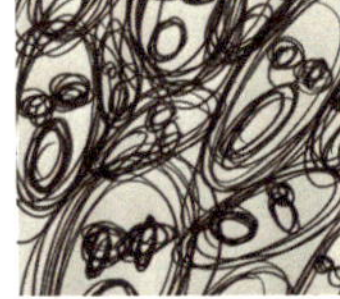

Mirror Mirror. The mirror doesn't speak back.

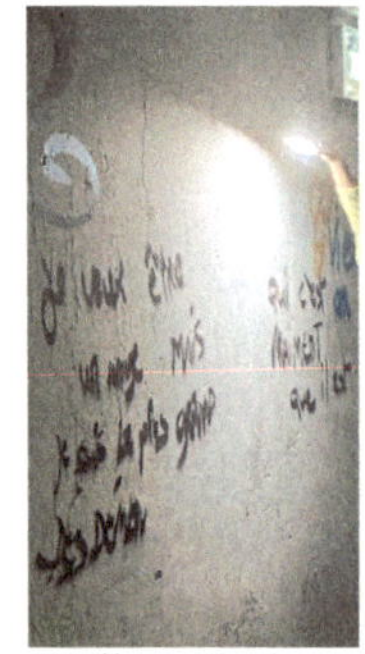

Wall marked by shadows. The message is for later.

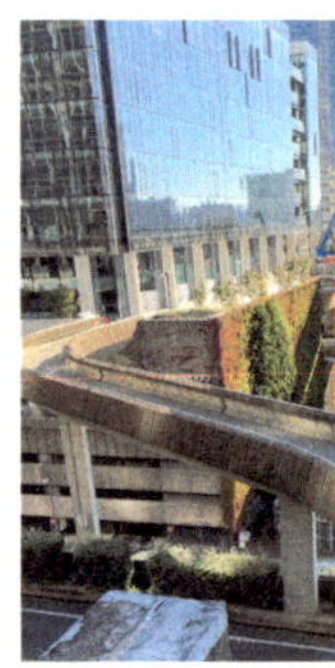

Footsteps are heard, but no one approaches.

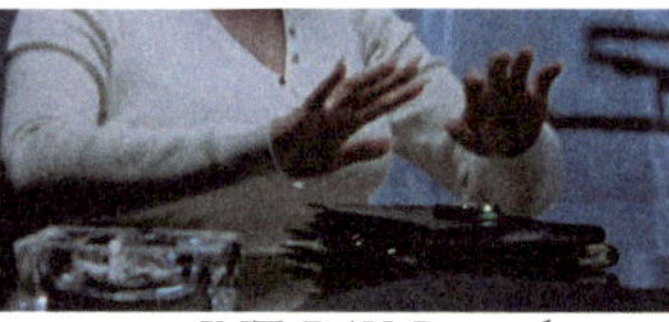

INT. DAY. Regret bureau.

EXT. HIGHWAY. The city bleeds through concrete.

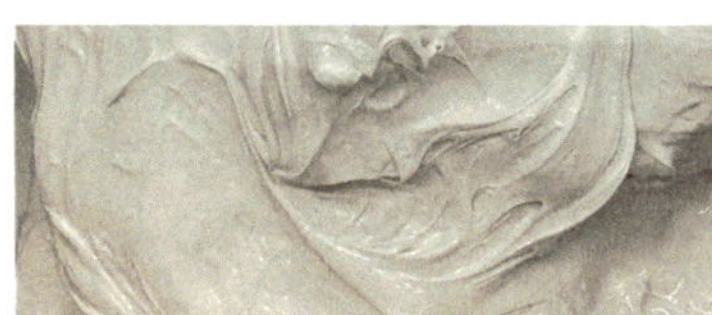

Marble shouldn't feel this cold.

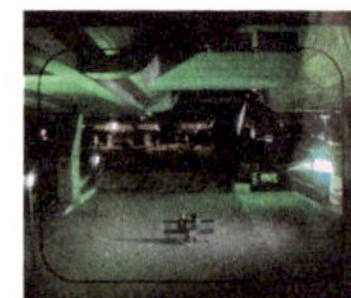

INT. NIGHT. Darkroom. The stage is gone.

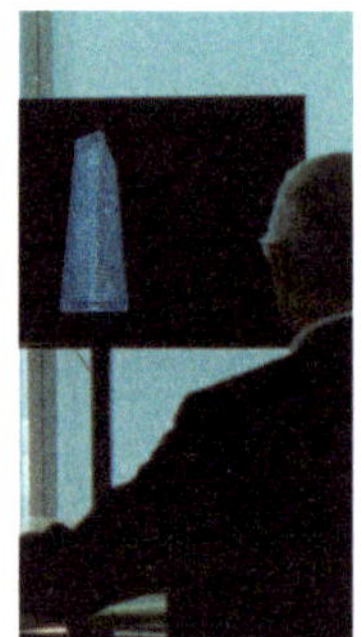

Behind the glass, an arm moves, too slowly to be human.

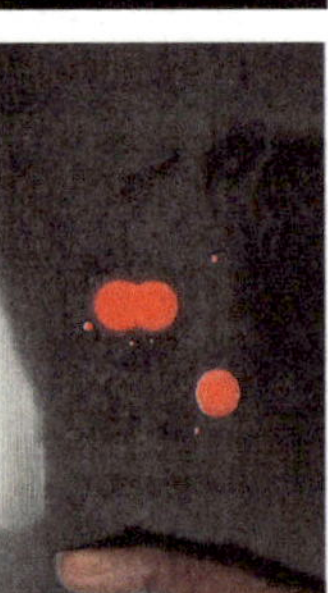

Two red dots at the end of the corridor. Push the button.

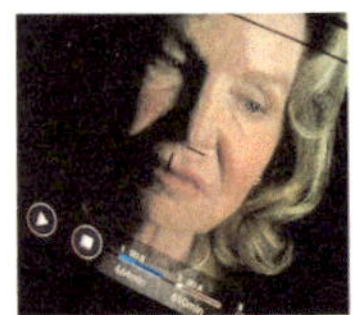

A mask that hides NOTHING.

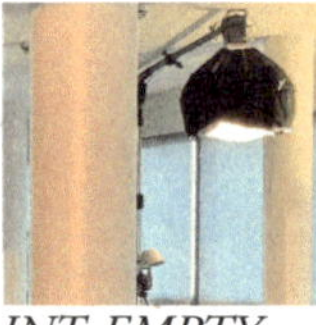

INT. EMPTY OFFICE. A man looks at a curtainless window. Rear window.

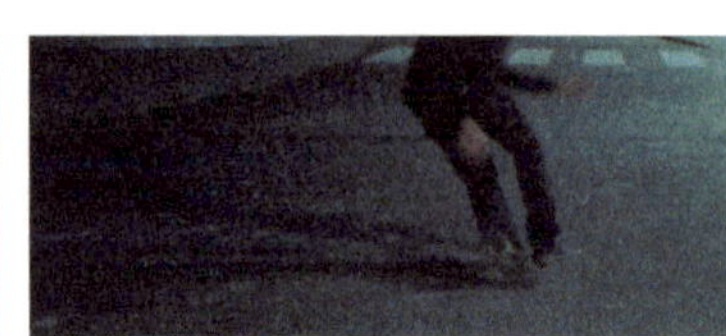

INT. BALLROOM. Silence has a shape.

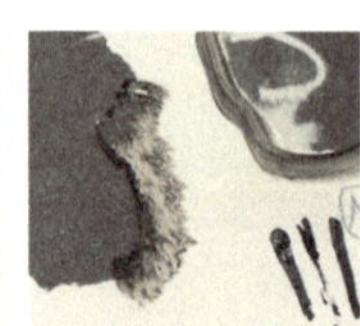

Fixed camera, long shot.

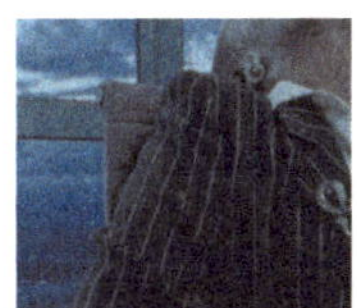

They built it
to resist time.

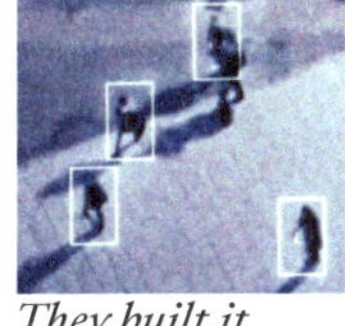

From the 31st
floor, you could
see everything.

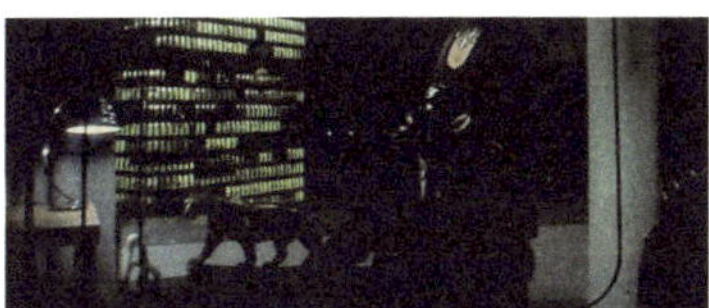

La Défense,
January. The
signage started to
glitch.

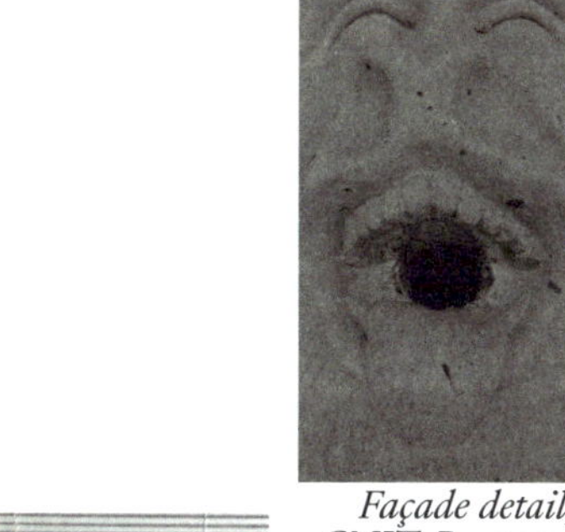

Façade detail,
CNIT. Rumored
to represent
the architect's
mother.

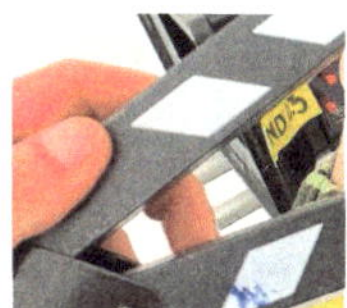

To be identified.

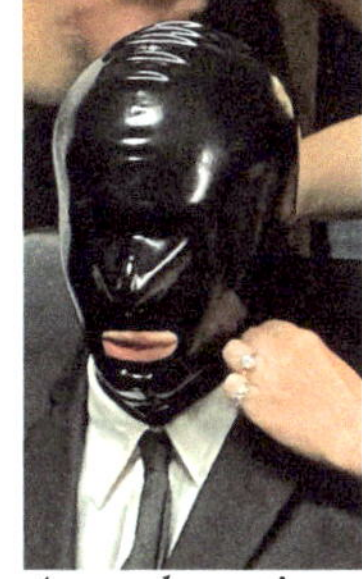

Annual meeting,
Tower A. Dress
code: unreadable.

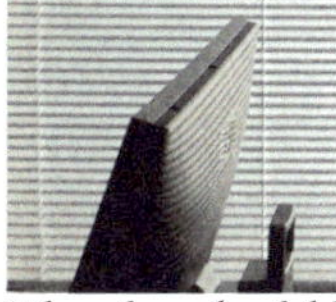

They found a folder named "STAGE
DESIGN." Inside:
94 photos of BDSM.

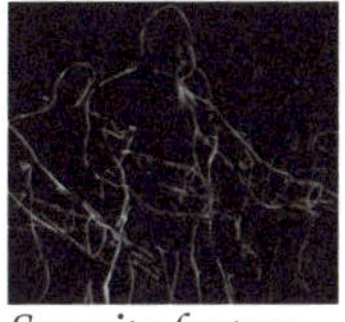

Security footage.

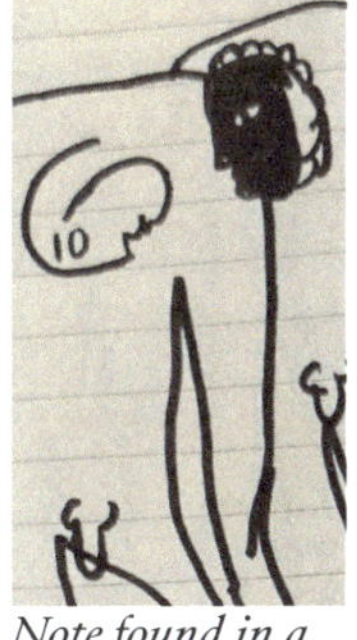

Note found in a
notebook in the
underground of
La Défense.

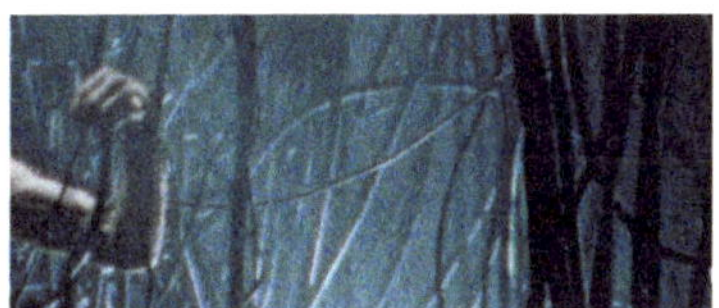

No windows. No Wi-Fi.
Just regrets.

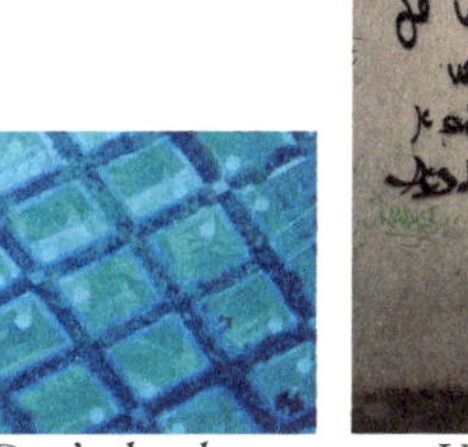

Don't they know
it's the end of the
world?

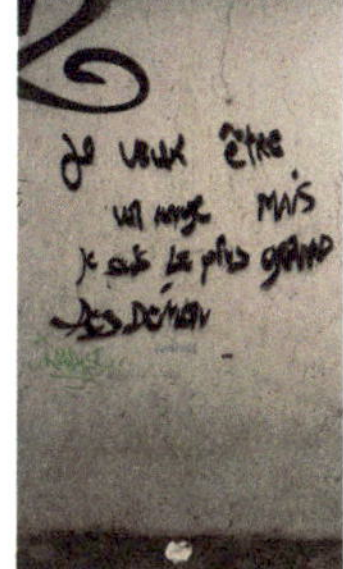

Underground
passage near
the RER B.
Traces of sperm
on the wall.

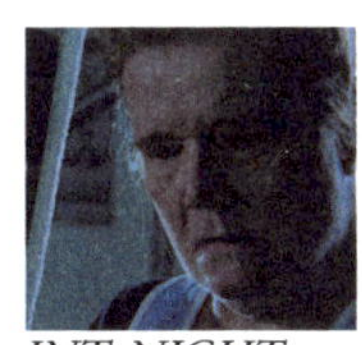

INT. NIGHT.
Tears.

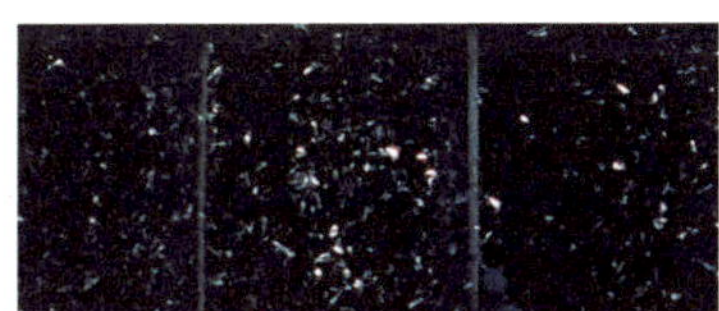

A child drowned
here in 1994.

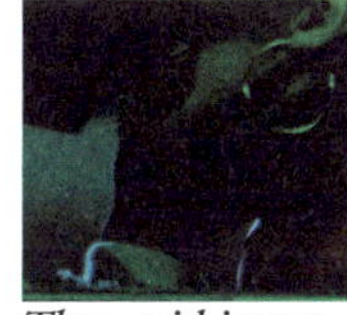

They said it was
art therapy.

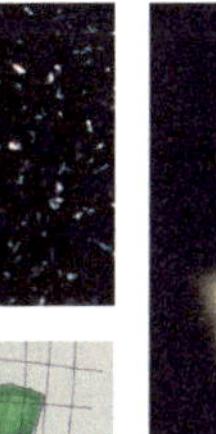

He drew the same
face again and
again.

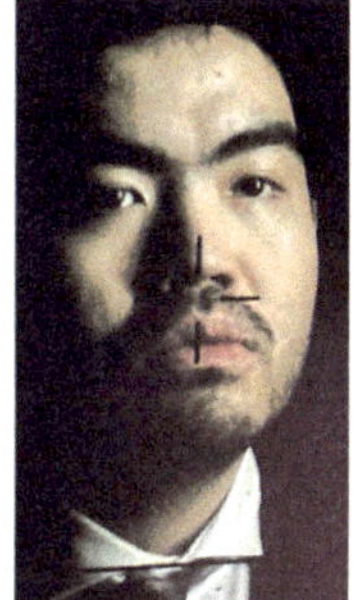

He worked in
finance. But
the suit was for
someone else.

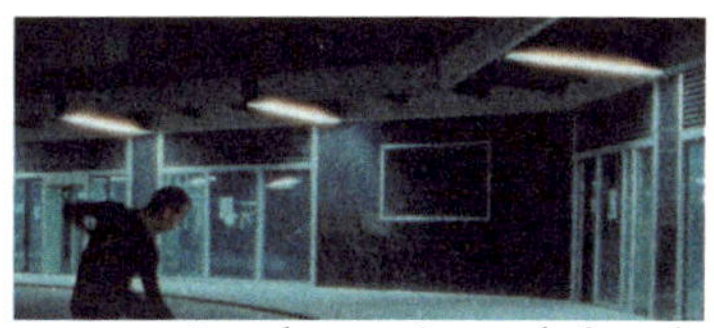

Last known image before the
blackout. Nobody can identify
the man.

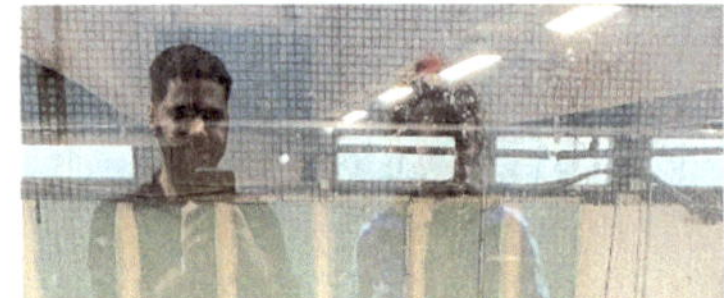

Selfie before the second day of shooting.

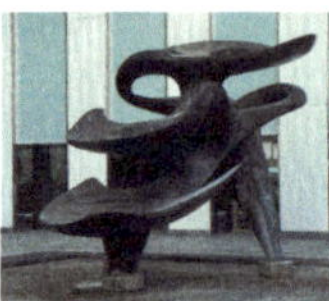

Sculpture. Originally installed to block a sniper's line of sight.

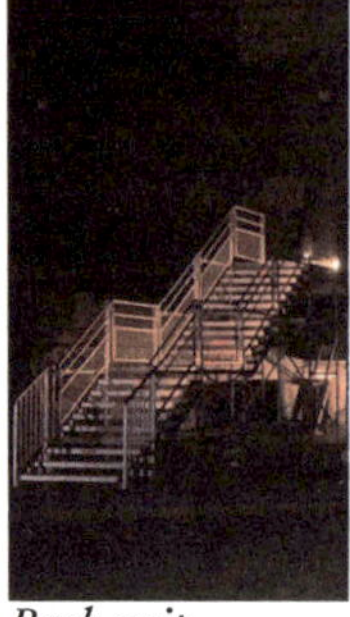

Back exit, Tower E. Used once, never again.

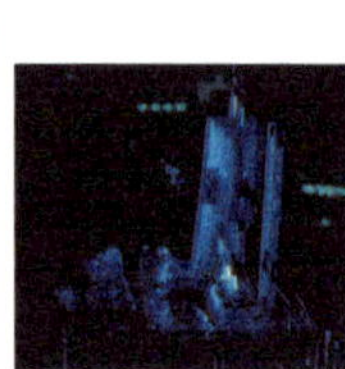

Like a prayer.

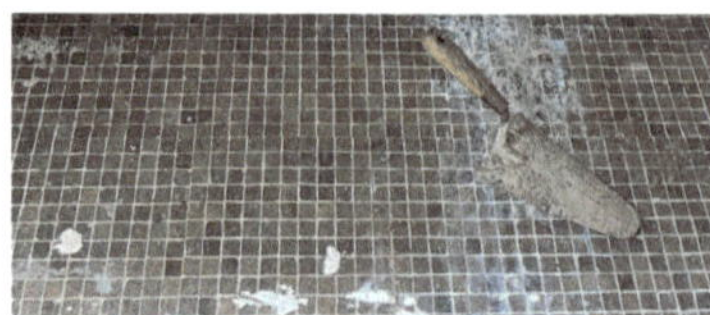

Ceiling of the old tunnel beneath Esplanade. Some say it ends at l'Élysée.

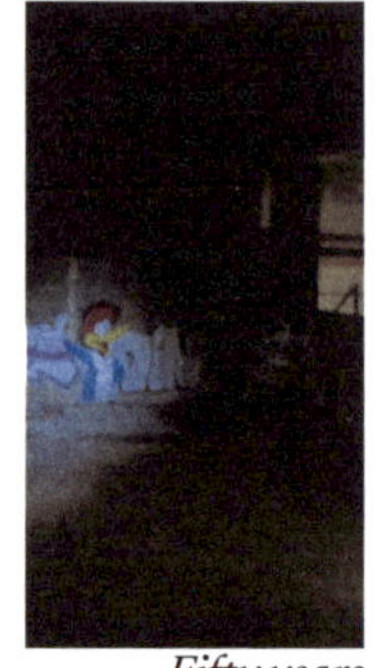

Fifty years of silence.

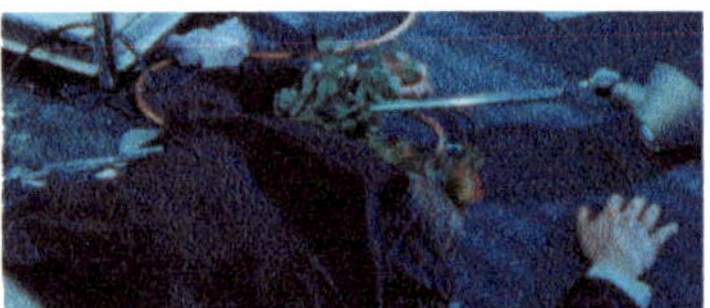

Take 3, action.

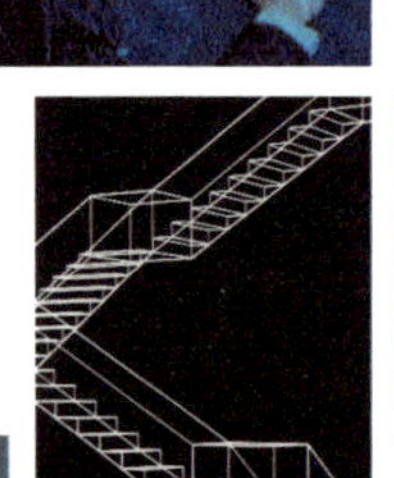

Dreamlike stairs to the Pacific Club.

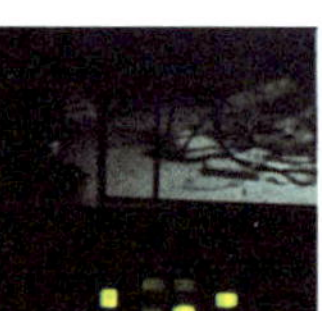

Fake news.

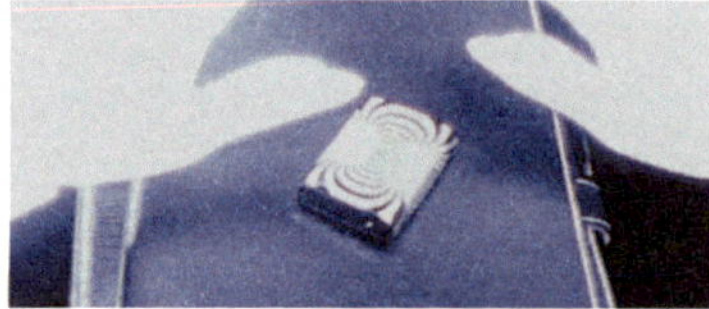

Exposure: voluntary.

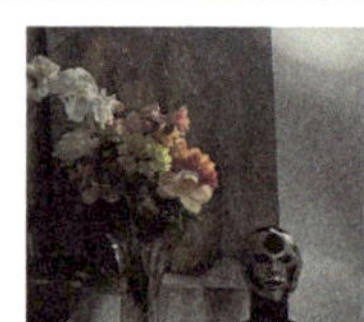

La Défense Hospital, waiting room.

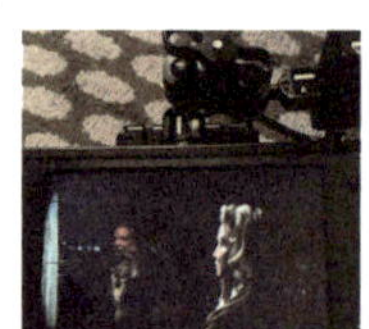

Hush...Hush, Sweet Charlotte.

Ghost of Charles de Gaulle.

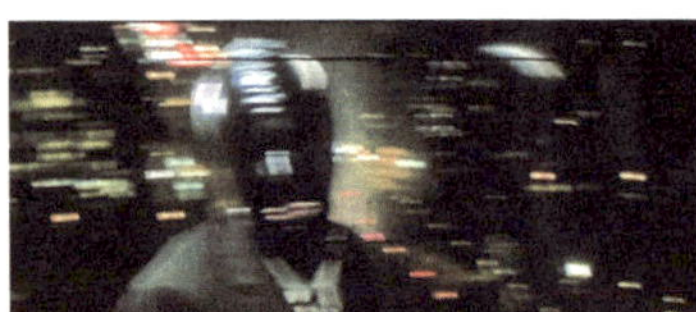

He loved her too much.

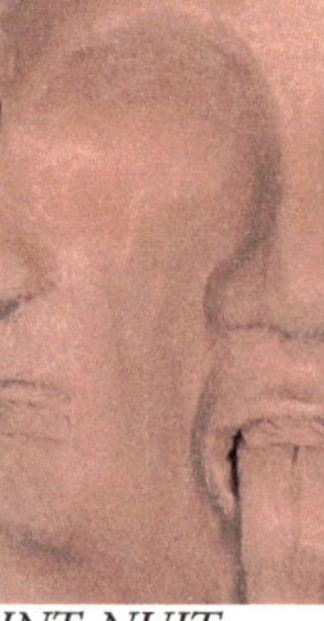

INT. NUIT. HILTON LA DÉFENSE

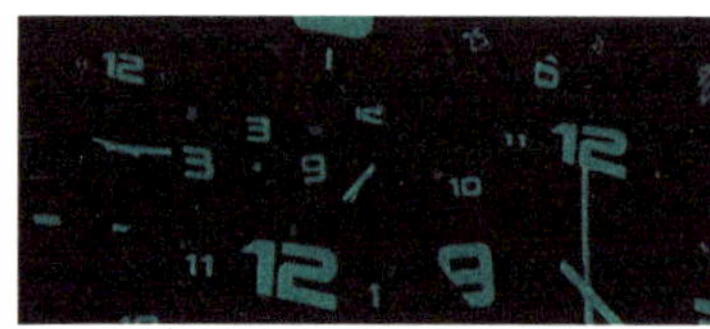

Four minutes to save the world.

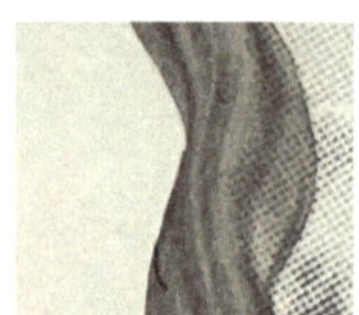

Cropped black and white image of a lost building.

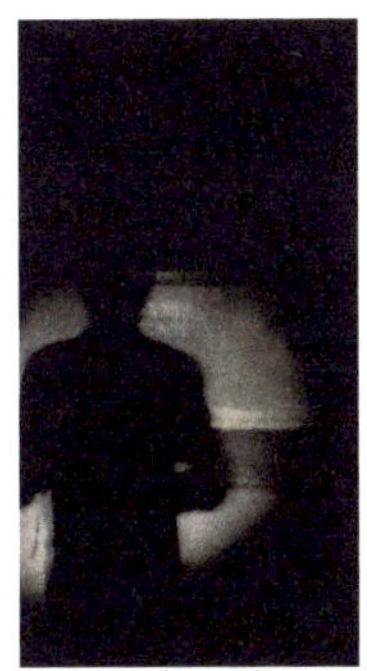

Somewhere beneath the Tour Atlantique, files are still being updated on men declared dead in 1962.

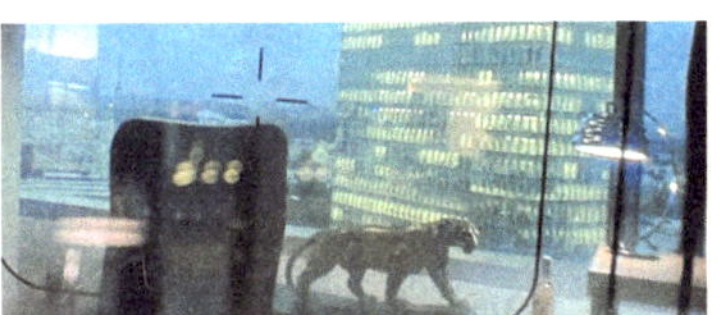

Paris is just a mirage they built around the Obélisque. The real city is offshore.

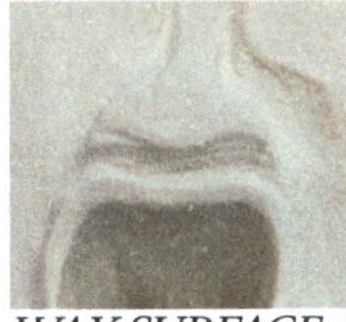

WAX SURFACE / FLESH TEXTURE / MARBLE VEIN

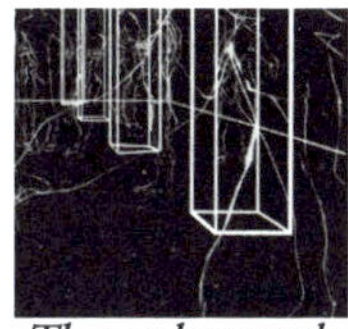

They rehearse the trials of former colonies. The verdict is always the same: procedural error.

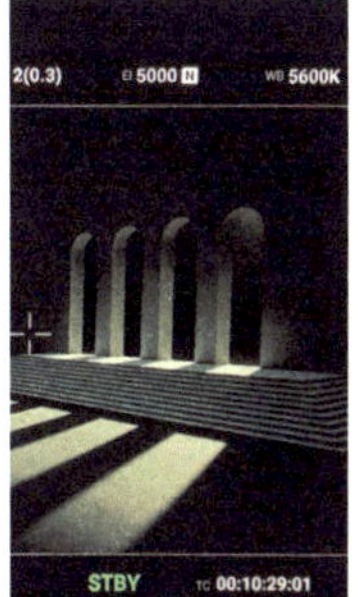

She watches the news. The war is always in the Middle East.

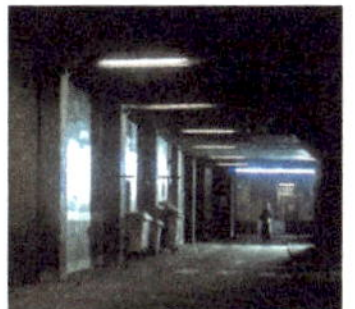

Sodomy in the basement of La Défense.

Not in the plans. Only accessible with Algerian blood.

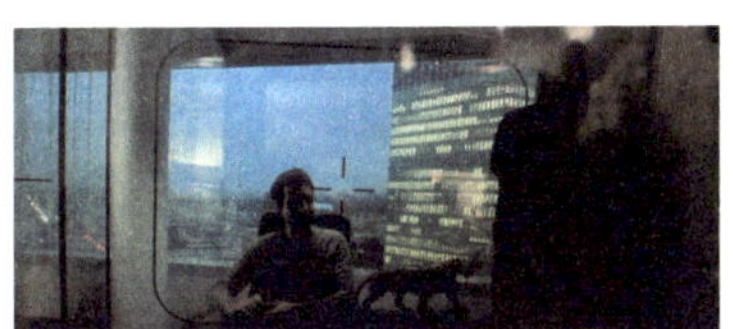

A film with Alain Delon plays in the background.

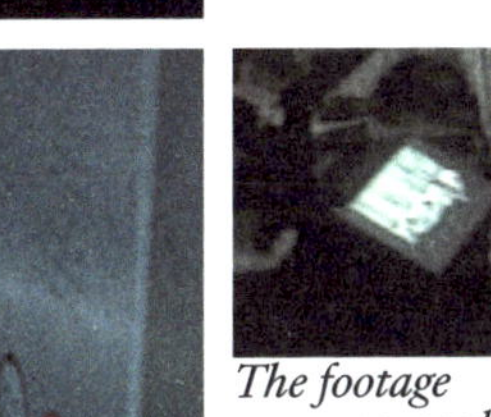

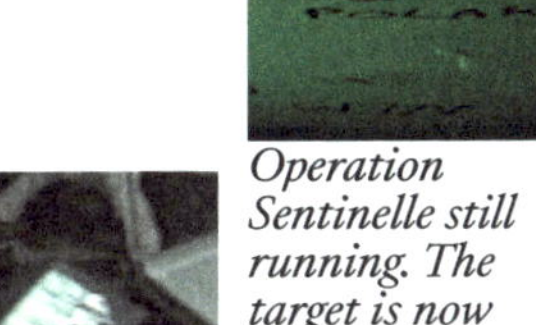

Operation Sentinelle still running. The target is now metaphysical.

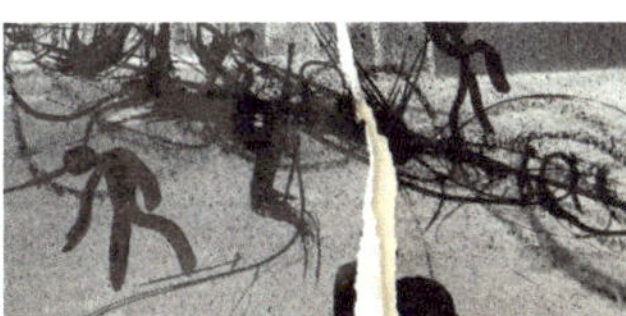

Genderless, tireless, fluent in French republican values.

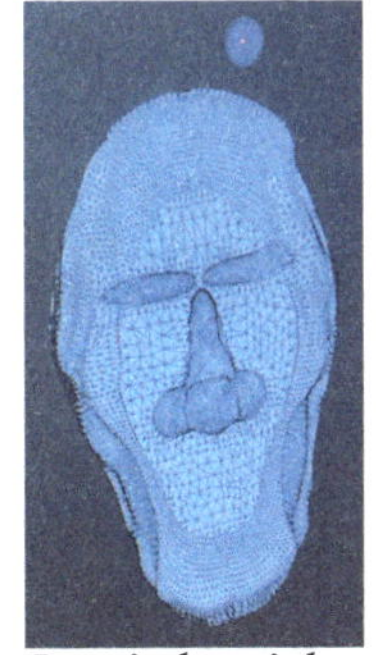

Post-industrial martyrdom.

The higher it goes, the less time passes.

The footage was recovered from a burnt server beneath Courbevoie.

A million roses for Karl Marx

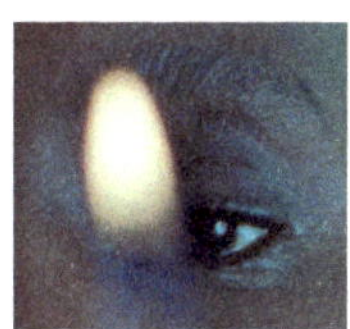

EXT. NIGHT— FIRE FIRE FIRE

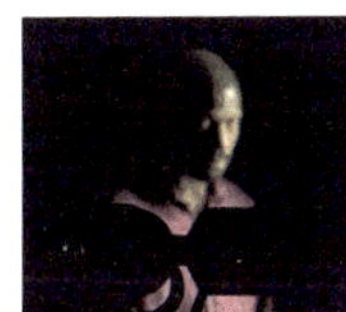

Blue turned grey, the white remained immaculate. The red turned brown.

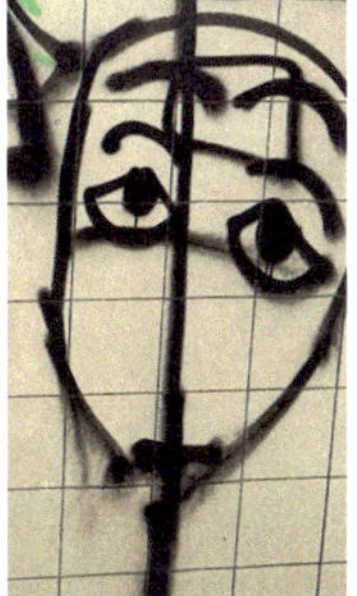

The ghost of a disappeared banlieue. Drawn by a student who spoke Wolof and disappeared after curfew.

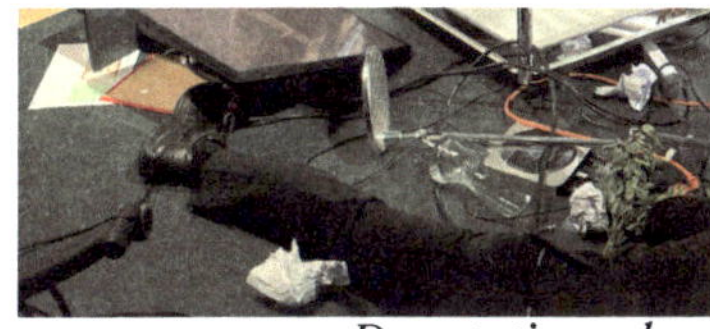

Deportation orders.

Data?

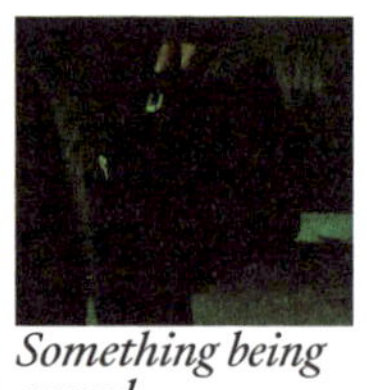

Something being
erased.

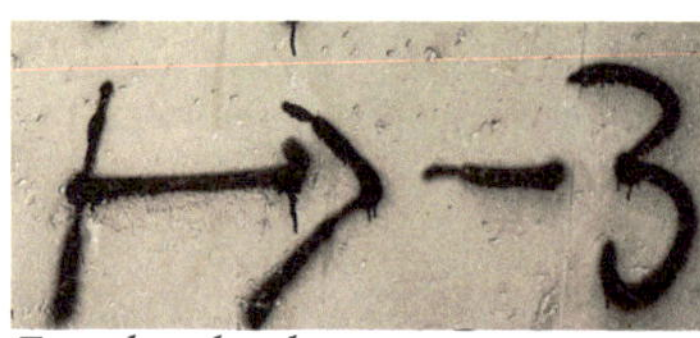

No
windows.
Only simulations.

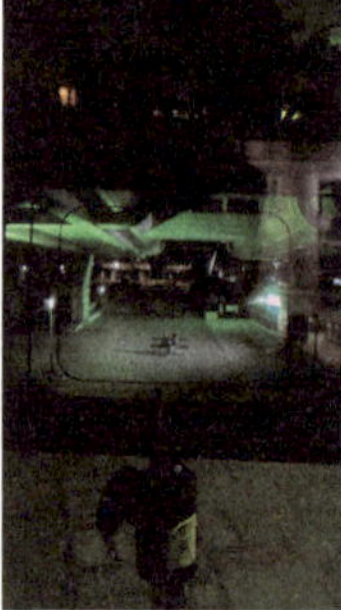

A building with
all the archives.

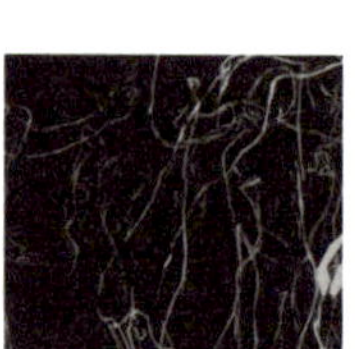

The floor, after
the shock.

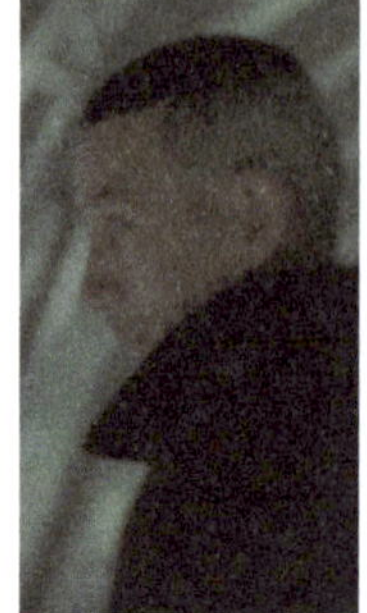

EXT. NUIT.
Silence.

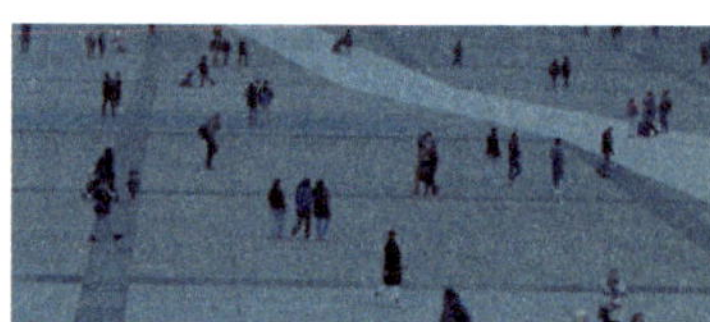

A person
supervises drones
tracking migrants
near the RER.

Found under the
mall Les Quatre
Temps.

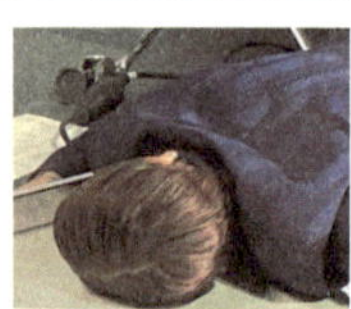

INT. DAY. Riots.

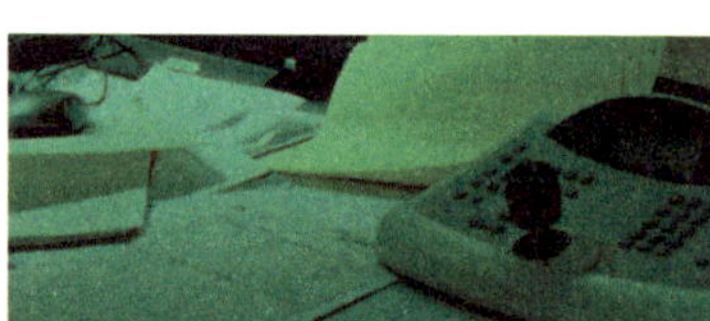

This was once a public square.

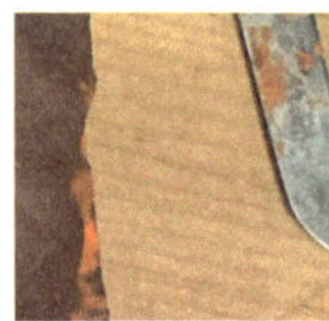

Better the devil,
you know.

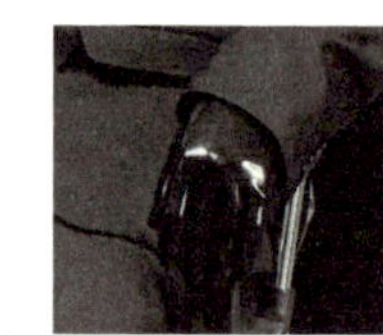

It was the hand of a private security
agent in a luxury gallery, trained to
detect "non-normative behaviors."

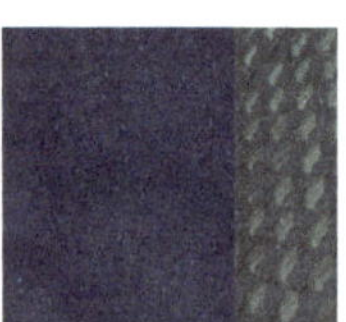

Tourists smile—
they say "cheese."

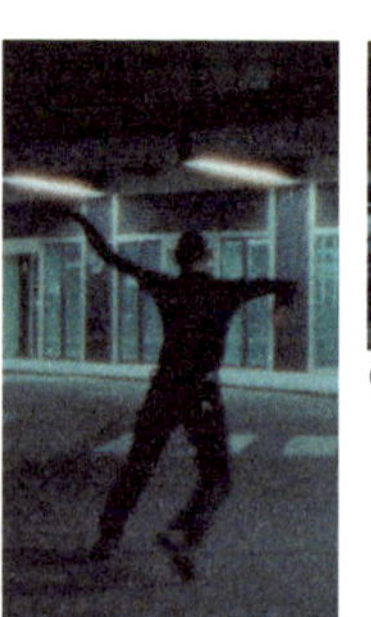

Camera obscura.

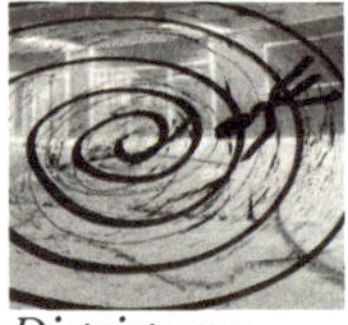

Districts are
drawn like cages.

He believed his body could forecast
market collapses.
His back pain aligned with
the CAC 40.

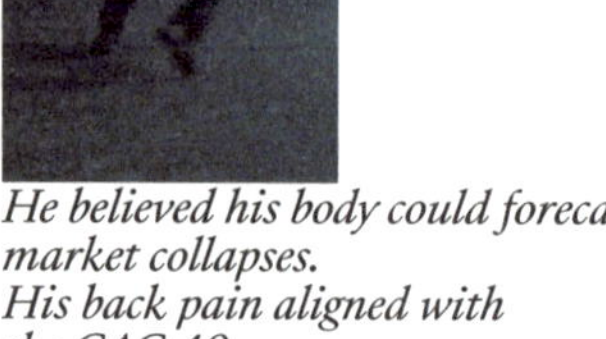

She entered the
lobby at 11:06.
The footage ends
there.

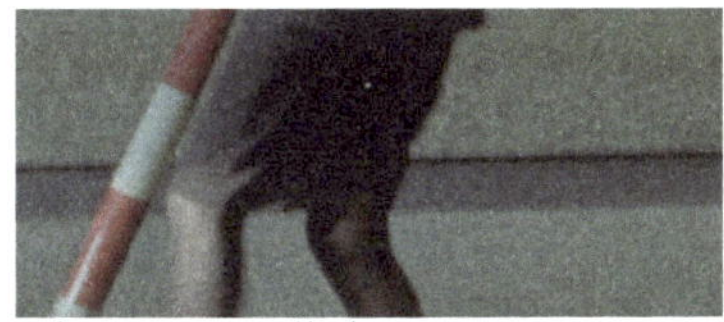

The street smelled like detergent and piss.

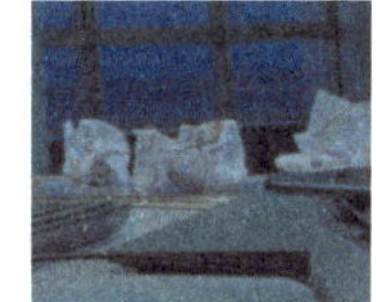

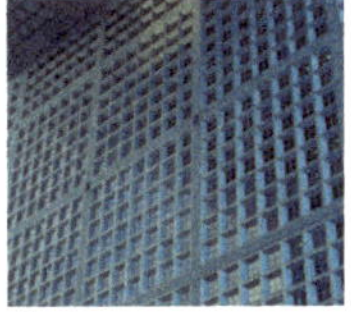

Ants.

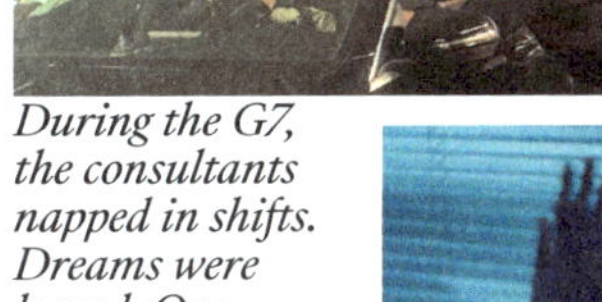

During the G7, the consultants napped in shifts. Dreams were logged. One predicted a coup.

INT. ESPLANADE DE LA DÉFENSE– RIOT DAY

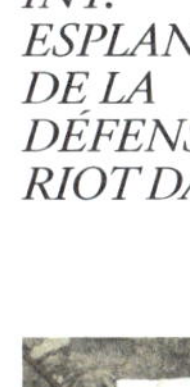

Each window hides a room with a different god.

Bloodline.

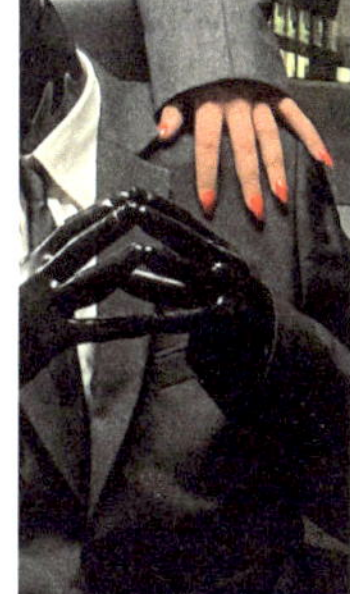

A gesture of love or liquidation.

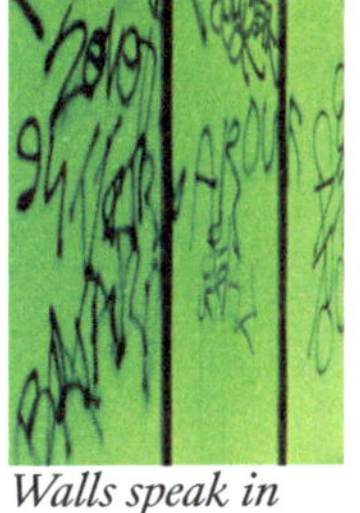

He stares into the camera. He's been down there for days.

Walls speak in tags. This one says: "France is a fiction financed by concrete."

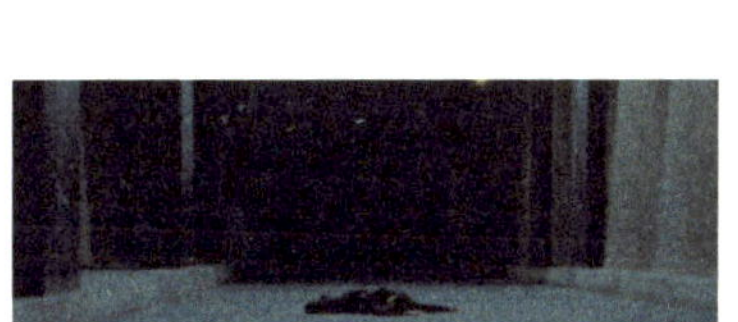

He threw himself through the windshield during a seminar. Said the Holy Spirit told him to.

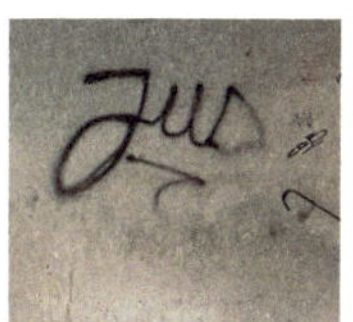

Underneath, a lipstick kiss.

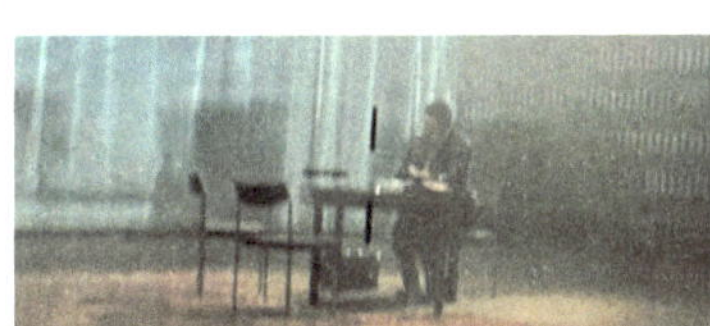

A locked door behind the CNIT archives. It only opens when the market crashes.

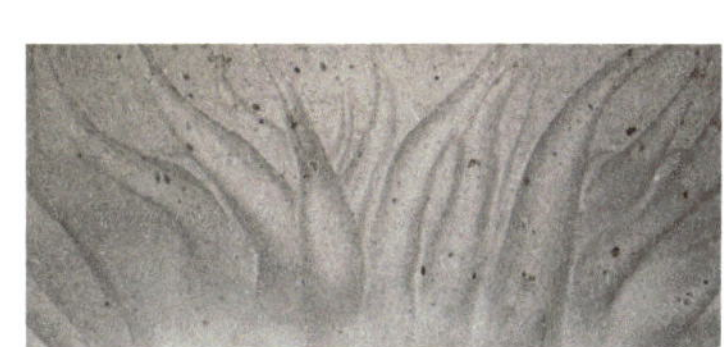

Looks like veins.

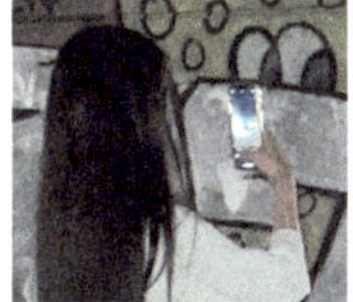

Beds made for people who never sleep. Meeting at 3 a.m., file sent at 3:02, coffee at 3:17.

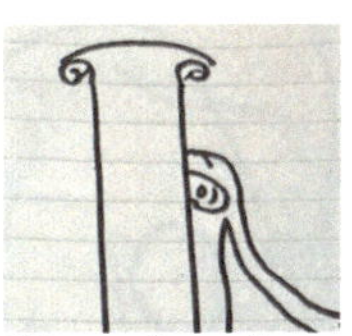

He unplugged every screen on his floor.

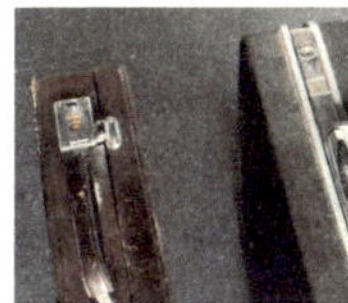

The evangelist touched it and said: he has risen among the bankers.

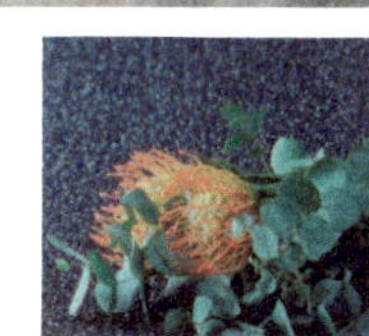

The unknown soldier.

LA DÉFENSE TRILOGY

Produced by Manon Messiant – Iliade&Films with

*LA DÉFENSE I –
PACIFIC CLUB*

Azedine Benabdelmoumene
Taos Bertrand
Julien Mézence

*LA DÉFENSE II –
TO EXIST UNDER
PERMANENT SUSPICION*

Kayije Kagamé

*LA DÉFENSE III –
DEMONS TO DIAMONDS*

Kayije Kagamé
Denis Lavant
Alexandra Stewart
Loubna Abidar
Alain Chaillot
Meliana Roman Gamboa
Elyjah Timera
Adam Sinclair
Wei Yang
Erwan Kepoa Falé
Anne Benoit
Félix Maritaud
Eva Huault
Pierre Demones

Published in conjunction with the exhibition

PANTHEON

Kunsthalle Basel
February 15–May 25, 2025

Curated by Mohamed Almusibli

The film *La Défense Volume III - Demons to Diamonds*, 2025, is commissioned by Kunsthalle Basel, in partnership with Lo schermo dell'arte with FRAC Bretagne, Visio production Fund, Florence, and the Vega Fondation, Toronto.

Supported by Doha Film Institute, le Centre national du cinéma et de l'image animée (CNC), The Renaissance Society, Chicago (Renaissance TV), Lafayette Anticipations – Fonds de dotation Famille Moulin, Paris.

This project was selected by the Fondation des Artistes' patronage committee, which gave it its support.

Valentin Noujaïm's exhibition at Kunsthalle Basel was supported with an in-kind contribution from Options (Switzerland) Ltd.

The mediation projects were realized through the generous support of the Art Mentor Foundation Lucerne, the Thomas and Doris Ammann Foundation, and the Canton of Basel-Stadt.

Kunsthalle Basel and Valentin Noujaïm wish to thank Marc Attallah, Negar Azimi, Azedine Benabdelmoumene, Taos Bertrand, Leonardo Bigazzi, Alex Brack, Billy Bultheel, Baptiste Caccia, David Camarou, Barbara Casavecchia, Sophie Cavoulacos, Antoine Cormier, Christiana Demetriou, Pierre Demones, Pauline Doméjean, Simon Gérard, Victor Gouteyron, Adam HajYahia, Peter Handschin, Martin Hatebur, Camille Houzé, Mirco Joao-Pedro, Kayije Kagamé, Olivier Magnier, Manon Messiant, Simon Muller, Edwin Nasr, Oswaldo Nicoletti, Stephan Pestalozzi, Raphaël Raynaud, Chloé Royer, Space Afrika, François Tessier, Laura Windhager, Lemlem Zemulu, Nicolas Pirus, and the technical and artistic teams involved in the trilogy.

Kunsthalle Basel
Steinenberg 7
4051 Basel
Switzerland

kunsthallebasel.ch
info@kunsthallebasel.ch

Kunsthalle Basel Team during *Valentin Noujaïm: PANTHEON*

Director and Chief Curator: Mohamed Almusibli; *Head of Administration:* Medea Chiabotti, Jenni Schmitt; *Head of Exhibitions:* Lena Katharina Reuter; *Curatorial Assistant:* Yana Kadykova; *Head of Technical Department:* Reinhard Pelger; *Head of Communication and Events:* Sina Bauer; *Communication and Events:* Vera Oberholzer; *Head of Art Mediation:* Desirée Hieronimus; *Art Mediation:* Lale Keyhani, Ananda Schmidt; *Head of Publications and Bookshop:* Clarisse Fahrtmann; *Photo Archive:* Giulia Ficco, Layla Jenni; *Administration:* Mara Berger, Claire Schneemann; *Exhibition Technicians:* Tom Senn (Deputy Head), Elena Gerosa, David Häring, Uwe Walther; *Library:* Lionne Saluz; *Head of Visitor and Supervisory Services:* Maximilian Rück, Semaya Mehret (Deputy Head), Ophélie Cabanero, Irina Choffat

Kunsthalle Basel / Basler Kunstverein
is generously supported by
the Canton of Basel-Stadt.

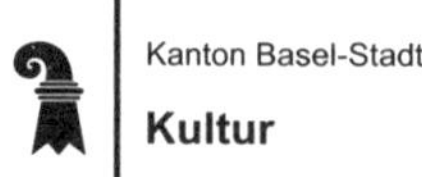

Valentin Noujaïm: INTERZONE

Editor
Mohamed Almusibli

Authors
Mohamed Almusibli, Perwana Nazif

Concept
Kim Coussée, Valentin Noujaïm

Graphic designer
Kim Coussée

Assistant designer
Maïlys Dütschler

Managing editor
Clarisse Fahrtmann

Publishing editor
Agnese Cantelmi, Mousse Publishing

Copyediting and proofreading
Lindsay Westbrook

All works by Valentin Noujaïm

First Edition: 2025
Printed by Grafiche Veneziane, Venice
ISBN 978-88-6749-705-8

€ 30 / $ 35

© 2025, Mousse Publishing, Kunsthalle
Basel, the artist, and the authors of the texts
Published and distributed
by Mousse Publishing
Contrappunto s.r.l.
via Pier Candido Decembrio 28,
20137, Milan, Italy
moussemagazine.it

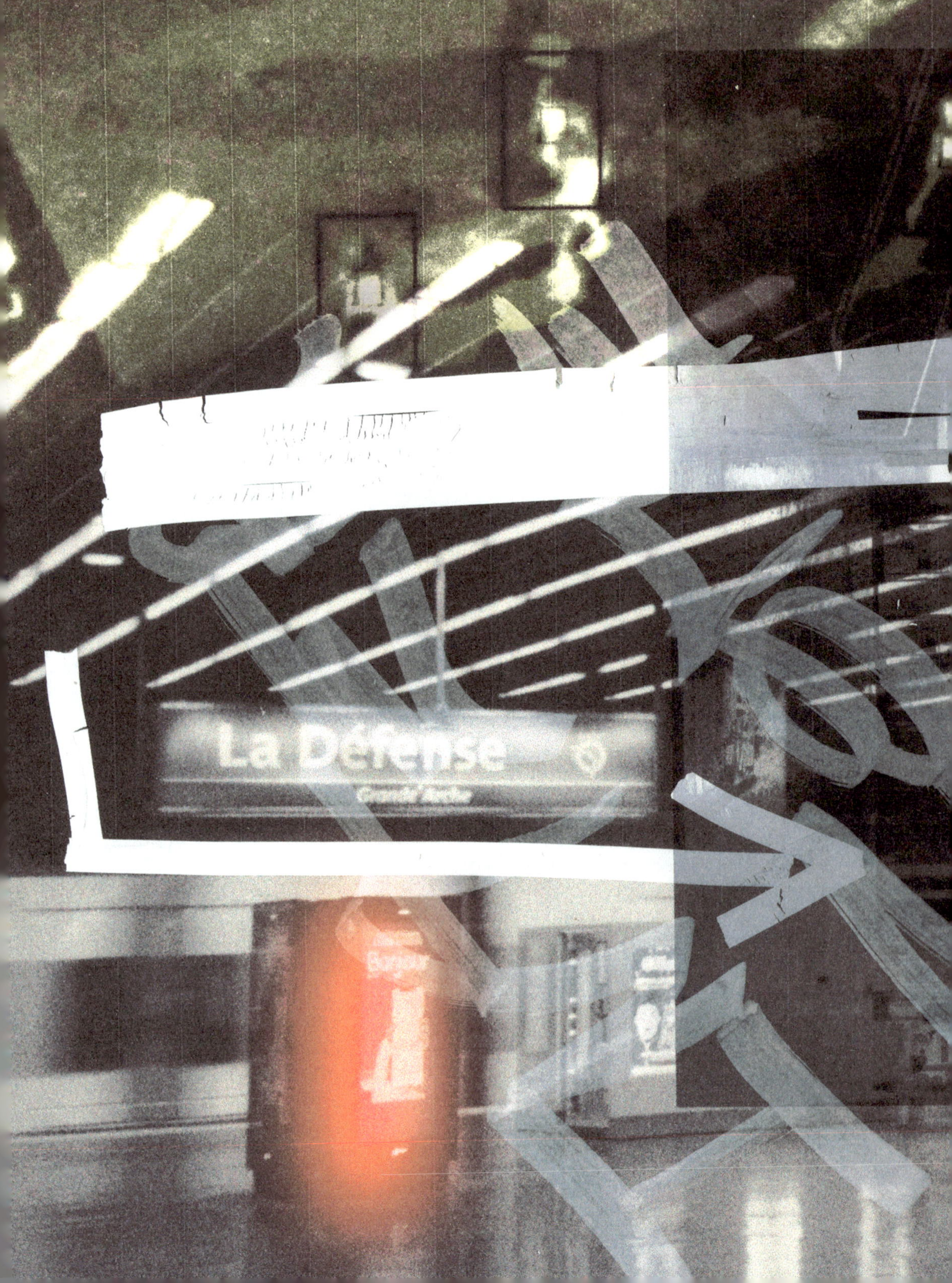
La Défense
Grande Arche
Bonjour

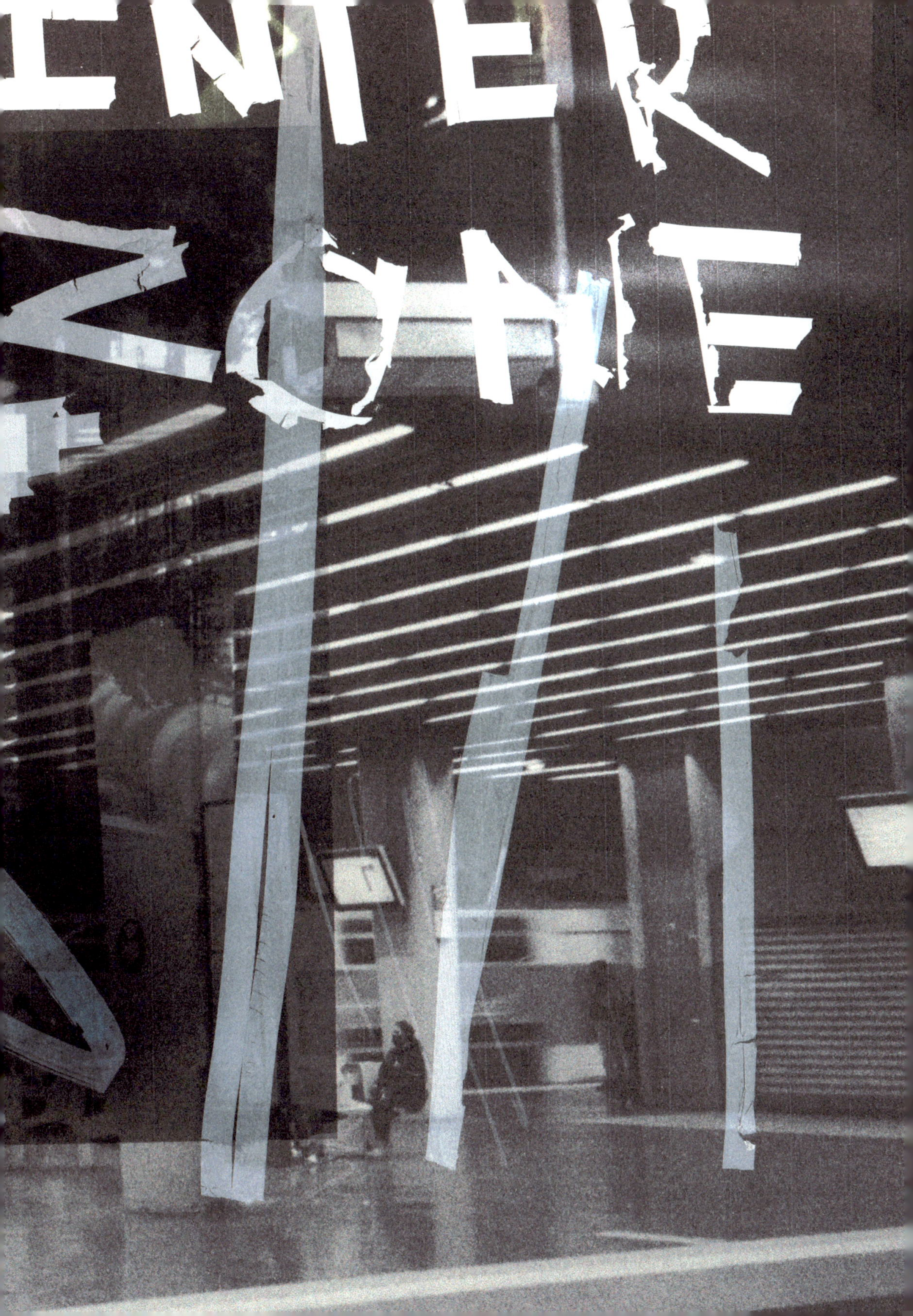
ENTER
ZONE